This is a long-overdue book! It c  in the power ministry of Late Rev ly beloved mentor. As a first-hand witness of the activities of Faith Clinic, I want to endorse as true all that is written in *The Faith Clinic Revival*. I believe it will correct wrong notions about deliverance ministry, and help to put in right perspective what ought to be. I salute the obedience of Tokunbo Emmanuel in yielding to the Holy Spirit to take up this project. I believe it will spur many to come up with more information that will be useful for future revision and expansion.

Rev. Victor G. Amosun, *Occupy World Outreach Ministries*

The *Full Gospel Business Men's Fellowship International* (FGBMFI) in the city of Ibadan rode on the crest of the ministry of Faith Clinic. We had common grounds in soul-winning, which was the primary focus of the FGBMFI.

This recognition of the works and times of Bro. Ibe speaks volumes about what it takes to be used mightily of God; which is far removed from what is generally understood and accepted today. The Church will be grateful for this work!

Pastor Alex Adegboye, *Senior Pastor, Stone Church, Ibadan*

Ibe (as he was popularly called) mixed an intense focus on Jesus Christ with a love and compassion for all people, which made him an ideal disciple of our Lord... His place in the Church is not easy to fill and his contagious love of the Lord, difficult to duplicate.

Professor Bill Isaacs-Sodeye, *Author, From Medicine to Miracles*

The powerful apostolic ministry of Faith Clinic, under the leadership of Dr. I.K.U. Ibeneme, was my foundation for ministry. If I have made any impact in life and ministry, I owe it to the grace of God, and the mighty move of His Spirit that happened in Faith Clinic. A big "Thank you" to Tokunbo Emmanuel for putting a few records of this great move in a book. I am sure Dr. Ibeneme, who has since joined the heavenly cloud of witnesses (Hebrews 12:1), will be pleased with this work.

Rev. Funke Adetuberu, *Women College of Ministry, Nigeria*

It gives me great pleasure to lend my voice to this highly commendable effort to document what great work our Lord Jesus did through our brother, Izuwanne Ibeneme, and the Faith Clinic group that he led in the Eighties.

I had known Brother Ibe, as he was fondly called, for many years. We were together in medical school. We were together in the Tuesday Fellowship group that met regularly at the Chapel of Resurrection. We were together at the UCH Christian Fellowship group.

Brother Ibe was a man who was very passionate about God and very, very passionate about making Him known. He was a quintessential witness who was very zealous for God and His glory. He carried the message of our Lord Jesus Christ all over Nigeria and overseas. His deliverance services opened the eyes of many to the reality of the unseen titanic struggle that goes on for the souls of men and women and the anointing God manifested through him set many a captive free.

This effort to document those heady days of love and power must be commended and it is my prayer that it will serve as stimulus to ginger many to the reality of what Almighty God can do through the willing and obedient.

Dr. Okey Onuzo, *Life Support Centre, Lagos*

I have carefully read the contents of this book, and as one who was so closely related to the late Dr. I.K.U Ibeneme, and also a part of the great move of God through Faith Clinic, I certify that the accounts in this book are true... The truth remains that Dr. Ibeneme was an apostle of deliverance. God used him to bring deliverance to the limelight, particularly in Nigeria, and generally in Africa. Tokunbo Emmanuel must be commended for the good job of putting the move of God at Faith Clinic into writing as directed by the Holy Spirit. I recommend this book as a must-read book for people who love the truth and want to study about the deliverance revival movement that broke in Nigeria from the 1980s.

Bishop Marcus Benson, *ICOF Continental Bishop of Europe, Ireland*

THE
FAITH CLINIC
REVIVAL

Eyewitness accounts of the move of God through Faith Clinic Nigeria Inc. and the ministry of Dr. I.K.U. Ibeneme

TOKUNBO EMMANUEL

Raising the voice of Wisdom!

The Faith Clinic Revival
Copyright © 2013 by Adetokunbo Emmanuel

Published by
SOPHOS Books
163 Warbank Crescent
Croydon
CR0 0AZ
United Kingdom

Unless otherwise stated, all Scripture quotations are taken from
the *King James Version* of the Bible.

ISBN 978-1-905669-48-6

Cover design by *Tope Enoch*
Printed in the EU

CONTENTS

In memory of
Late Dr. I.K.U. Ibeneme (1946-1993).
Eternity will unveil the whole story...

AUTHOR'S PREFACE

Sometime in the year 2006, the Lord ministered to me that I needed to write a book about the spiritual awakening that happened through Faith Clinic Nigeria Inc. and the ministry of Late Dr. I.K.U. Ibeneme. My spirit registered the instruction but I did not immediately do anything by way of execution. The only action I took, about a year later, was to share the idea with Rev. Victor Amosun, one of the key ministers at Faith Clinic in those days. I had met him at a meeting held at *Cornerstone Christian Centre* in Bromley (UK). On informing him of the mandate to write, he agreed it was a much-needed project and promised to help in any way he could.

Two years passed without any further action on my part. By December 2009, three days to the end of that year, the Lord impressed it upon me again, this time more strongly. He insisted that the Faith Clinic story must be told. I could no longer shrug the consciousness of this assignment aside. When I asked the Lord why He was keen about this work, He said to me: "All my moves upon the Earth are documented, first in Heaven and then on the Earth. There are records of this move in Heaven but none yet on the Earth."

That did it! I committed myself to obeying the Lord's command and just over three years later, the book you are now reading is the result.

It has not been a straightforward process because many of the participants during the revival have since moved on to different ministries, vocations and geographical locations. Yet, the will to write found a way to connect with some who would most certainly have personal stories to share about the movement. I had to depend on these because there was not much available, as the Lord had said, in terms of existing records.

I am grateful to God for entrusting me with such a holy assignment. I had no credentials other than my calling as a scribe in His Kingdom,[1] and probably, the fact that I was, as a teenager, an eyewitness of the glory of God that permeated the Faith Clinic era. I became born-again in that dispensation and soon afterwards, began to manifest consistently the authority to cast out devils — the spiritual phenomenon that Faith Clinic was widely known for.[2]

With joy in my heart, therefore, much gratitude to God, and a deep sense of awe, I present *The Faith Clinic Revival*, to the One "from whom the whole family in heaven and earth is named;" I present it to "the general assembly and church of the firstborn who are registered in heaven." May this work glorify the Father and accomplish all that He had in mind when He sowed the seed in my heart; may it inspire a generation towards a closer walk with God and dedicated service in His glorious Kingdom.

ACKNOWLEDGEMENTS

Father, thank you! This calling is a great honour indeed. Your Spirit helped me all the way. My prayer for this work now remains: *O Lord, use it for your glory and let thy Kingdom come!*

Many thanks to Sis. Ego Ibeneme, Bro. Ibe's widow, who after quizzing me a number of times, gave her blessing for this project.

I am greatly indebted to all the *Faith Clinic* ministers that I was able to interview (I cannot, for space constraints, mention you all by name). You are true heroes of faith who are still waging a good warfare for the Lord. Your reward with the Father shall be great indeed!

I am grateful for the input of many of Bro. Ibe's contemporaries that I was able to contact. Thanks for the interview time, endorsements, suggestions and encouragement.

Thanks to everyone from whose written works I have quoted freely (please find details in the *Notes* section). Sources include Ayodeji Abodunde's book, Remi Tejumola's book and blog posts, Aunty Christie

Ifebueme's book, Professor Bill Isaacs-Sodeye's book, Jackson Ekwegum's magazine, Akinwale Johnson's unpublished manuscript and Tope Mene's Bible School notes. Special thanks to Ella Verkalk, of the African Studies Centre Library in Netherlands, for sending me a copy *Sade's Testimony* at no charge.[1]

Many thanks to the *Books With A Mission* staff and team for their valuable input: Sis. Bimpe Odusan for proof-reading; Tope Enoch for the cover. Special thanks to Abraham and Tope Lordson for their moral support throughout; to Pastor Sola Mene, and countless others who, aware of the ongoing project, lifted me up in prayer; to my friends in the UK for being there; to Bro. Kola Akeredolu for his kind assistance; to my mother, Pastor Esther Olulaja for constantly asking, "How far with the book?"

Lastly, I couldn't have done this without my family; my dear wife, Linda, and precious children: Destiny, Daniel and David. You mean so much to me. Thanks for standing with me even when the pursuit of this assignment meant living many miles apart for a season — a very long season. It was a sacrifice worth making. Thank you for believing in me. I'm loving you every passing day!

Father, once again, thanks! Let the name of Jesus Christ be glorified both now and forever. Amen.

FOREWORD

The book you are about to read is a most unusual book. It is about a child of the Most High God, Dr. I.K.U. Ibeneme, who led a team of believers to wreck havoc on the kingdom of darkness, on the platform of a ministry known as *Faith Clinic*. The book is about compassion for people; tenacity in ministering to the needs of others until the final solution is reached; the display of the awesome power of God. *The Faith Clinic Revival* is about leadership and team-work. It is about humility, love and simplicity.

Bro. I.K.U. Ibeneme was my friend for many years until his *home call* in 1993. I saw the characteristics described above in him from close quarters over the years—while we were students at UI and after our student days. Bro. Ibe was in all respects a "commando" for Jesus. He could penetrate most obstacles men put up to preach the gospel. Bro. Ibe poured out his life on the altar of service. He spent and was spent for the gospel. He did not serve for fame or gain. He had ample opportunity for both, but *for him to live was Christ*.

At Faith Clinic, human vessels positioned themselves to be mightily used by God. Faith Clinic was truly a "move of God," and some of the stories in this book are absolutely breath-taking. Satan's wickedness is massively exposed, as well as the awesome power of God to set men free. Some of the accounts are very weird. Really bizarre. You may be left wondering, could this be real? People vomiting office pins, lizards etc; a lady giving birth to a coconut; items disappearing from a wardrobe etc. Well, trying to evaluate spiritual issues with natural reasoning will always end in a deadlock. Spiritual things can only be decoded spiritually.[1] We are wrestling against *"spiritual wickedness in high places."*[2] This is not kid's stuff!

Just as God works mighty miracles, the devil also works "mighty miracles." God's miracles bless people; satan's "miracles" enslave and destroy people. This is what this account portrays. May I remind us, though, that God and satan are not involved in a struggle for supremacy. Jesus said "I saw satan *fall like lightening* from heaven."[3] His defeat was SWIFT! Jesus disarmed principalities and powers (period).[4] This book portrays that in essence.

We owe the author, Brother Tokunbo Emmanuel, loads of gratitude for taking the time and putting in the efforts required to put this work together. *You have added greatly to our body of knowledge. Your efforts will never go unrewarded.*

Happy reading!

- *Rev. Emiko Amotsuka*

INTRODUCTION

W hat are the marks of a true revival? When can we say authoritatively that a season of spiritual awakening in any region is an authentic move of God? Without gainsaying, the ministry of Faith Clinic during its heydays had the hallmark of a divine move of God's Spirit. It was an awakening that served a specific purpose in the timeline of God's workings.

I am using the word "revival" here in a general sense to mean an awakening to spiritual reality that has a direct impact on the eternal destiny of man, the transformation of his character, his experiences of God and the domain in which he exists. I am also, for the purposes of this account, using it interchangeably with the phrase "move of God." After all, every revival is a move of God but not all moves of God are necessarily revivals.

Going by the insights of Jonathan Edwards, the great revivalist and theologian of the eighteenth century, who was used by God during the Great Awakening in New England (1734-1746), the marks of a true revival include the following:

- It glorifies Jesus Christ.
- It attacks the powers of darkness.
- It exalts the holy Scriptures.
- It lifts up sound doctrine.
- It promotes love to God and man.[1]

This account of the ministry of Faith Clinic will show that the events that gradually took centre-stage in the city of Ibadan, Western Nigeria, from 1983 to 1993 fulfil these criteria. Jesus Christ, not man, was the central focus of the ministry of Faith Clinic. Attacking the powers of darkness through the frequent casting out of demons was a major feature. The holy Scriptures were exalted as the supreme authority that settles all matters. Sound doctrine was promoted through the messages and the Bible School. Love for God and man was demonstrated in practical ways through the selfless service of ministers in the movement.

Further traits of revival throughout Church History include:

- Large numbers of conversions.
- The sovereignty of God over the movement.
- A central human vessel used of God as a catalyst for the revival.
- Occasional physical manifestations of the touch of God in the lives of seekers.
- Some extremes and excesses.
- Opposition to the move from various quarters.

Again, all these were regular features of Faith Clinic. Unprecedented numbers of people got saved during the

Faith Clinic years. From its beginnings to the time it peaked, it was obvious that God was the One at work in Faith Clinic. While Christ was the focus, the Lord used a human vessel in the person of Dr. I.K.U. Ibeneme to fuel the revival. There were many visible manifestations that accompanied the touch of God, mainly in the area of deliverance (or exorcism). Being a relatively "new" experience in the Church of Nigeria at the time, which some struggled to contextualise appropriately, there were some criticism and opposition from a number of quarters. This book will further expound on these themes.

As we look back at the development of this movement, I consider it helpful that we use the comparative attributes listed above to ascertain or question its legitimacy. That the revival waves have receded is not enough reason to discount its legitimacy. Just as every other occurrence that have generally been acknowledged as revivals, the Faith Clinic revival had a starting point, a peak and a decline.

THE AZUSA PARALLEL

As a further comparison, I decided to examine the Faith Clinic revival alongside another widely-acclaimed awakening – the Azusa Street revival of the early twentieth century (1906–1914). Apart from the fact that this historical revival fulfils the aforementioned features, it also made a distinct contribution to the Body of Christ. God used the Azusa outpouring to restore back to the Church in wholesale fashion, the knowledge and experience of the Baptism of the Spirit with the accompanying manifestation of speaking in tongues. Prior to the ministry of William J. Seymour (1870-1922), a principal figure during this revival, reports of believers speaking in tongues were few and far between. Yet there was a growing hunger for the encounter among believers.

Similarly, before Faith Clinic Nigeria Inc. started in 1983, very little was known about the process and practice of casting out of devils. This was certainly the case within the Church in Nigeria. No doubt, there were isolated cases in various places, but God used Faith Clinic to establish this spiritual reality on a church-wide basis. Just as the Azusa Street revival is regarded as the father of modern-day Pentecostalism, we can safely say (and many have said) that the Faith Clinic revival was the father of the modern-day deliverance ministry in Nigeria.[2]

THE DEARTH OF DOCUMENTATION

Unfortunately, the Faith Clinic revival took place in a region of the world where the art of documenting events is not yet an ingrained culture. Considering the scale of what happened in and through Faith Clinic, our book-shops should be full of writings about the move, whether for or against! This would most certainly have been the case if the Faith Clinic revival happened in the Western world.

Perhaps conditioned by this absence of a writing-and-documenting culture, those who were central to the move did not concern themselves with capturing, recording or archiving the events as they occurred, as powerful as they were. Apart from the fact that they were busy almost round the clock, they probably considered it prideful to engage in such perceived "self-promotion."[3] Until Dr. Ibeneme went to be with the Lord in May 1993, the few writings he had done were not circulated widely.[4] Others did not take it upon themselves to share his insights abroad or spread the unfolding events at Faith Clinic to the world through the print or audio-visual media. Contrast this with the many documentations of Frank Bartleman during the Azusa outpouring,[5] or *The Apostolic Faith* newspaper that the Azusa mission circulated to thousands of people,[6] or the criticisms of the Los Angeles Daily Times that labelled the move "a new sect of fanatics."[7] William Seymour also wrote a book, *The Doctrines and Discipline of the Apostolic Faith Mission*, as a resource for the churches that the mission birthed.[8] All these materials are not only accessible today, they provide firsthand insight into this historical movement for those who want to investigate or gain inspiration from it.

Perhaps we can excuse the failure to write about the Faith Clinic movement as an oversight. The ministers were unreservedly engrossed with preaching the gospel and casting out devils. In fact, they admittedly shied away from any obsession to take pictures or keep records of the great things that God was doing—and many of the pictures or records that existed are hard to come by today.[9] This notwithstanding, it is an oversight that has deprived the younger generation of valuable information and spiritual impetus. Many young people today have not even heard about the awesome things that God did at Faith Clinic or that there was once a minister in Nigeria called "Dr. I.K.U. Ibeneme." This became glaring to me when I began the research for this work – almost nothing was available in written or audio form.

My determination to obey God and write about Faith Clinic increased after I noticed its unexplainable absence from two major works that chronicle the development of Christianity in Nigeria—*End-Time Army: Charismatic Movements in Modern Nigeria* by Matthews Ojo[10] and *A Heritage of Faith: A History of Christianity in Nigeria* by Ayodeji Abodunde.[11] How could they have missed even a casual mention of Dr. Ibeneme or Faith Clinic Nigeria Inc.? Again, I consider these omissions excusable over-sights, since both works relied heavily on available documentations.[12]

I, therefore, had to rely heavily on the recollections of people who witnessed the revival (thus the subtitle); people who played key roles during the Faith Clinic move – at least, the people I could locate. There were many more people I could not meet, ministers and those who were ministered to. Thankfully, I was an eyewitness too, so were my father, mother and siblings. Where necessary, therefore, I have given my personal accounts (particularly in the notes). I confess that I could not write as an uninitiated historian! My hope is that this work will provoke and unearth further accounts.[13]

Setting out, I started a blog about Faith Clinic[14] and also created a Facebook page[15] with the hope of attracting some attention and create an interest in the work. I also began to find a few references to and written accounts about Faith Clinic that proved helpful. I have tried to prioritise these writings because they do not only add further authenticity to the eyewitness accounts, they remind us, I hope, of the benefit in capturing events as they happen. All credits to cited material are given in the notes at the end of the book. The notes also contain further helpful commentary. (I have intentionally moved these supplementary comments from the main text in order to maintain a continuous reading experience).

Far from being a mere historical treatise or an academic exercise, I hope *The Faith Clinic Revival* is received as a testimony of God's awesome power displayed amongst us in the not-too-distant past. Some of the accounts are almost unbelievable! God truly did unusual miracles during the Faith Clinic revival and through his servant, Bro. Ibe.

Moreover, I hope this work will prove to be an acknowledgement of a move that influenced an entire generation of believers in Nigeria; a worthy recognition of a man that God used in a unique way; and an inspiration for those who long for God to move amongst us once again.

"Let this be written for the future generation."[16]

1

A WOMB FOR REVIVAL

Nigeria is a land that has benefitted from the moves of God. In diverse ways and through a variety of people, revival waves have swept through the land, just as waves of the sea sweep over the shore. The aftermaths of these are still around us today, from the schools built by foreign missionaries to the large congregations led by the ever-increasing, indigenous fruit of their labours.

In his well-researched book, *A Heritage of Faith: A History of Christianity in Nigeria*, Ayodeji Abodunde identifies six main movements that have shaped the nation's Christian landscape. Listed chronologically, they are:

- The Missionary Movement
- The African Church Movement
- The Prophetic/Healing Movement
- The Pentecostal Movement
- The Evangelical Movement
- The Charismatic Movement[1]

These six movements summarise the development of Christianity in Nigeria since the days of the foreign missionaries. Alongside the 19th Century exploration of West Africa through the Niger River and the ongoing trade of slaves, God used different missionaries to sow seeds of the gospel in the hearts of natives. Over time, these seeds began to take root in the ground with emerging works as the first fruit, including the Methodist Mission, Catholic Mission and the first African Bishop in the person of Ajayi Crowther.

As the early gospel work multiplied and the different missions experienced growth, there was a move that sought to establish the indigenous identity of the churches. Leadership was more or less wrestled out of the hands of the Europeans, either by peaceful transition or forced division. This paved the way for a more African expression of Christian worship. It also led to another strong move of God through native Nigerians.

God used men like Ayo Babalola and Moses Orimolade to spread the message of Christ with mighty signs. The healings and power demonstrations drew many to the Faith. Traditional religion was confronted and new missions started, including the *Cherubim and Seraphim Movement* and the *Christ Apostolic Church*.

These spiritual awakenings of the first half of the Twentieth Century produced thousands of Christians who began to learn the ways of God and develop a hunger for righteous living. There were also a number of growing movements that reached out to young people. These included the Scripture Union and the Student

Christian Movement. These movements naturally took root in the secondary and tertiary institutions.

University of Ibadan, which was started in 1957, was the first of the tertiary institutions. More were established around the nation in subsequent years, and it was only a matter of time before the fires of revival spread to the campuses, impacting the lives of many young people. Already, the Pentecostal fires that were lit during the Azusa Street revival were sweeping the globe. They reached the Nigerian church like a thunderbolt and many sought for the baptism of the Holy Spirit. God used the veteran missionary, Pa S.G. Elton, as a catalyst to spread the message and experience of Pentecost throughout the country, especially among University students.[2]

The Pentecostal revival was very powerful on campuses in the 1970s. Many groups and fellowships experienced moves of God that are still reverberating to this day. Notable among these groups in the University of Ibadan were the IVCU and the Tuesday Fellowship. Bro. Ibeneme, whom the Lord will later use to start Faith Clinic Nigeria Inc., was a student in UI during this time. He was also involved in both fellowships.

IBENEME, THE STUDENT

Izuwanne Ibeneme had already encountered Christ and become a believer while a student at the Federal School of Science in Lagos. He gained admission into the University of Ibadan in 1971 to study Medicine. Throughout his stay on campus, he was a member of IVCU and also active in the Tuesday Fellowship.

Emiko Amotsuka, also a student in UI at this time, met Bro. Ibe at the Tuesday Fellowship and became closely acquainted with him. They were both involved in the fellowship at leadership levels.

Bro. Emiko recalls, with a sense of awe, the move of God that took place at the Tuesday Fellowship during their time on campus:

> The experiences we had at the Tuesday Fellowship were so sacred. The involvement of the power of God was so much. God did so much among us that it will scare me to put myself in the picture.[3]

As a typical Pentecostal fellowship, there was much worship, prophecy, prayers for the sick, and praying in the spirit with other tongues. Bro. Ibe's love and zeal for God were evident from those early days. He had a passion for souls and would go to any length to reach people for Christ.

Bro. Ibe had a way of wrangling through hostile environments to preach the gospel. In the early 1970s, those who had experienced the baptism of the Holy Spirit were in the minority, and they were often looked upon with suspicion, especially by the so-called orthodox churches. But in spite of the stiff opposition to the gospel and Pentecostal message (unlike today when many 'orthodox churches' are now gospel-oriented), Bro. Ibe would always find a way to overcome the hurdles and preach the gospel of Christ. "That was something uncanny about him," Bro. Emiko remembers. He was driven by compassion for the lost and did not want anyone to miss hearing the gospel. He would do anything to reach out to people and introduce them to the love of Christ.[4]

Matthew Owojaiye, also a leader in the Tuesday Fellowship, has recollections of those times and how Bro. Ibe was zealous for God.

> As students and leaders of the Tuesday Fellowship, our college degrees meant nothing to us. We were sold out to God. We would go from village to village, preaching the good news. We will pray for the sick (in hospitals) on Sunday and go back on Wednesday to check whether they have been discharged. We were tenacious and determined.
>
> Bro. Ibe was mad for Jesus. He ministered selflessly for God and did not receive money for it. He was not motivated by monetary gain...
>
> I once took Bro. Ibe to my village for evangelism. Many of the people that came out of that meeting are now Permanent Secretaries. I locked myself in the room praying while Bro. Ibe preached. It was when he gave the altar call that I came out. Many children responded but I drove them back. This happened twice. By the third time, the Lord said to me, leave them alone. Today, many of them are doing well for the Lord.[5]

The zeal that Bro. Ibe had for the things of God touched the life of students and lecturers alike. Professor Bill Isaacs-Sodeye, in his book *From Medicine to Miracles*, made reference to the influence of Bro. Ibe that led to the rededication of his life to Christ. He was a Senior Lecturer in the University of Ibadan at this time (1973). He was also a compromised Christian who had dabbled into the occult, was addicted to alcohol and indulged regularly in extra-marital affairs. He once had a three-month dealing with one of his students, but after feeling guilty of ruining the young lady's life, he broke off the relationship. The lady, subsequently, suffered a nervous breakdown and left the University for six weeks.

Professor Isaacs-Sodeye recounts in his book:

> When she returned, she ran into an evangelist who was a student of mine. She had a thorough conversion experience and desired that I should taste it too. That young man (now a specialist gynaecologist) came with the girl at night to watch me play squash, and to initiate discussions. Dr. Ibeneme (for that was his name) was respectful as he was persistent.
>
> A day came when my partner failed to turn up and Ibe (as he was called) got his chance.
>
> "Can I have a word with you outside, sir?" he asked. I wanted to get rid of him, so I went out to meet them.
>
> "Sir," he said, "this lady knows your life story. She is sure you have no peace, even though you go to church. If you really have Jesus, sir, you would have peace." He opened his Bible and read Romans 5:1 and expounded it, relating it to other passages.
>
> Somehow, it made a strange impact on me. I decided to take a holiday to examine the proposition. Taking holidays was not a habit I indulged in. I believed I needed every day for scientific research. But this was too important. If that young man was

right (and he sounded as if he had first-hand experience to back up his witness), it could change my
life.[6]

And it did! Professor Bill Isaacs-Sodeye went through
the Scriptures and found faith again. He testified in his
book: "I found peace as well. I came convinced, never to
waver again."[7] He would later be used of God to save
many souls and minister healing to the severely afflicted.

Professor Isaacs-Sodeye has this more to say about Bro.
Ibe:

> Ibe (as he was popularly called) mixed an intense
> focus on Jesus Christ, with a love and compassion
> for all people, which made him an ideal disciple of
> our Lord. Among other things, it made him (and he
> was very intelligent) neglect his studies at various
> times. Although he was my close friend and the one
> who was mightily used to bring me to the light of
> true salvation, this made me somewhat upset with
> him at times. My stance earned me a rebuke from
> the Lord in June 1975 and he was chosen to go, in
> my place, to the conference with the late David Du
> Plessis that summer. His place in the Church is not
> easy to fill and his contagious love of the Lord diffi-
> cult to duplicate.[8]

Adolphus Iteghie, who would later become one of the
ministers at Faith Clinic, was a staff of the University of
Ibadan bookshop in the early 1970s. He knew Bro. Ibe as
a leader in IVCU and the Tuesday Fellowship, and had
heard him speak during fellowship meetings. He
remembered that some of the brethren would sometimes

experience strange manifestations during worship, and the leaders of the revival often questioned what this was. Gradually, the phenomenon of casting out of devils started in the fellowship and prayers for deliverance began to feature from time to time.[9]

From these early days, God seemed to be preparing the young Ibe for a predetermined purpose, one that would come to pass in due course and affect thousands of lives.

FROM CAMPUS TO THE CITY

In a few years, many students who had experienced revival not only in UI, but also on other campuses across the country, graduated and took the fires of revival with them. The Lord used some to pioneer great works that are still with us today. Notable are the *Christ Chapel* movement through Dr. Chris Joda, a move that God used to spread the message of faith in the nation; the *Sword of the Spirit* movement through the young Francis Wale Oke that spread the fervour of evangelism and mass crusades; the *Rhema Chapel* movement through George Adegboye, another work that emphasised the Word of Faith teachings; *Calvary Production (CAPRO)*, through the efforts of Peter Ozodo and other graduates, the first indigenous mission agency from Nigeria that has raised and sent missionaries across Africa and beyond. The revival torrents from the campuses in the 70s; indeed divine workings of God in Nigeria that had begun many decades before then, was bearing fruit everywhere by the turn of the 80s.[10]

The Pentecostal and Charismatic revivals were waxing strong by this time. Encounters with the Spirit and the teachings of faith were taking root and multiplying in the life of the Church. The believers were speaking in tongues, understanding and confessing the Word, and reaching out to the lost. However, as great as these developments were, God, who was the One at work in the Church, had not yet finished restoring the truths of His Word in Nigeria. He would later single out Bro. Ibe as one through whom the revelation about the believers' authority over the activities of devils would be fully restored. In the course of time, the need for this spiritual understanding came to the fore.

THE CONVERSION AND DELIVERANCE OF ANSLEM MADUBUKO

The documented stories of Anslem Madubuko's conversion to Christ and how he eventually visited Faith Clinic for deliverance depicts the significance of what God did through Bro. Ibeneme and the ministry of Faith Clinic. It gives some insight into why, despite the great impact of the Pentecostal and Charismatic awakenings, God saw the need for a ministry like Faith Clinic — one that would open the eyes of the saints to the reality of the unseen realms and their authority in Christ.

Born to parents who all their lives worked in the educational sector, the young Anslem had a relatively pleasant upbringing. He was admitted to the University of Nigeria, Enugu campus, in 1976 and studied Architecture. Six years later, he graduated and moved to Lagos.

While still a student in Enugu, Anslem had become active in student politics. He also became a presenter on Radio Nigeria. He drove a car on campus and had everything going on nicely for him. By the age of twenty-one, he had gotten initiated into the Lodge society. As the first son of his father, a Lodge member, he had to join the fraternity. Anslem also associated himself with the Pirate confraternity and became a Capon (a leader) in his final year on campus.[11]

By the time Anslem was twenty-five, he had seen it all — drugs, women and occultism. But he was not happy. All of a sudden, he began to feel like he would soon die. He had become tired of life and could not make any sense of his existence. It was at this point that he had a dramatic salvation experience, and straightaway began to reach out to others with the message of salvation. His passion for God was undeniable. He joined Christ Chapel in Lagos and threw himself into the work of God. He did everything from ushering to evangelism to intercession. He was fully involved with the work at Christ Chapel

In spite of his unmistakeable conversion and unreserved commitment to the work of God, the young Anslem was enduring untold spiritual oppression. His past involvement with the occult caught up with him. He could not sleep well and had little inner peace. His eating patterns suffered greatly and he began to lose weight. Whenever he went to bed, he would experience terrible nightmares, which caused deep fear to reside inside him.

Helpless and confused, Anslem went to his pastor for help. The counsel he got was that he needed to stand on the word of God and make confessions of faith. He was told that he was totally delivered from demonic oppression by being a born-again Christian. His pastor was, of course, absolutely correct.[12] However, Anslem knew that he was still suffering; and this made him to ask many questions.

It was at this point in his life that the young Anslem learnt about Faith Clinic Nigeria Inc. He was advised to go and see a man of God, one Dr. I.K.U. Ibeneme, in Ibadan. Desperate for freedom, he travelled to Ibadan and attended the all-night programme at Faith Clinic. After prayers at Faith Clinic, Anslem was completely delivered, and for the first time since he gave his life to Christ, he had a perfect night's sleep!

"This is it!" Anslem said to himself. Thereafter, he began to lead people to Faith Clinic every weekend, everyone he knew who was suffering any form of spiritual oppression. He got close to Bro. Ibe and learnt a lot from the ministry of Faith Clinic. He was later invited to head the deliverance department of *Household of God*, the congregation Pastor Chris Okotie was starting at the time. That became an opportunity for him to reach out and minister to others.[13]

Today, Apostle Anslem Madubuko leads the thriving *Revival Assembly* in Lagos—a work that Bro. Ibe had the privilege of inaugurating in 1989.[14]

* * *

This account of the deliverance of Apostle Madubuko from spiritual oppression is significant because of the era in which it occurred — at the peak of the Charismatic move of God in Nigeria. It shows, to some extent, why God, in His wisdom, perhaps needed to raise a work like Faith Clinic. He needed to help the believers answer some of the questions they were having; and shed some light on some mysterious experiences that were defying logical explanation. For this purpose, God sought for and found a vessel in Bro. Ibeneme.

2

THE BIRTH OF A MOVEMENT

When we consider historical events that people have labelled "revivals", especially their beginnings, there is usually the evidence of God's sovereignty at work. In other words, these sustained phenomena are usually not pre-planned by the principal players. Indeed, God works through human vessels, like he did through William Seymour in the Azusa Street outpouring, but the vessels could not have told you in advance exactly what they would be used to do, how or when they would be used to do it. This partly explains the sense of suddenness and organic development in many of such revivals.

Upon close examination, however, we will discover an extended time of preparation that the vessel of God endured, a spiritual deficiency that needed to be addressed, a people desperate for the touch of God, and the readiness of God to transform the lives of men. Surely, known to God are all His works, and quite often, it is *after* He has accomplished them that they are fully known to us. This was certainly the case with Bro. Ibe and the work of Faith Clinic.

After his graduation from the University of Ibadan, Bro. Ibe did his National Youth Service in Kano, and later returned to the city of Ibadan. He got married to his wife, Sis. Ego, whom he had met while a student at the Federal School of Science in Lagos (they were also both medical students at the University of Ibadan and active in the Tuesday Fellowship). Bro. Ibe specialised in gynaecology and began serving as a doctor in the University College Hospital (UCH).[1]

The young Ibe's fervour for the things of God did not wane after he left the University environment. He continued to be involved in the Christian community as a leader and minister of God's word. Long before Victor Amosun got close to Bro. Ibe through Faith Clinic, he was accustomed to his ministry in other fellowships.

> My contact with Dr I.K.U Ibeneme dates back to 1981 or thereabout, through conferences, seminars and Sunday services on the campus, either in IVCU or The Polytechnic, Ibadan. One of the special areas he handled was "Courtship, Engagement, Wedding and Marriage." I remember brethren used to have challenges with the traditional wedding, in relation to engagement lists and other traditional stuff. His teachings were so practical and enlightening; he made people see the spiritual implications of those elements. I think from that time I had been warming up to him, even though it never crossed my mind that I will work with him in ministry.[2]

PASSION AND COMPASSION

Being a person with an insatiable passion for souls, Bro. Ibe seldom missed an opportunity to minister to people and lead them to Christ. He had a heart of compassion towards his patients and always took time to listen to their ordeals. Many of these patients were women who were having fertility problems – a situation that was not only common in Nigeria, but also, owing to the cultural expectations of family and community, burdensome for the women involved. Many of them were under much societal pressure and were desperate for solutions. Naturally, Bro. Ibe would counsel them and go all out to give the best medical treatment possible.

It was in the course of counselling his patients that Bro. Ibe began to discover that some of the infertility conditions were not responding to medical treatment. Prescriptions that sorted out the issues of some were completely ineffective when used by others with similar symptoms. Also, when medical examinations were carried out, they usually showed that everything was normal and there was no medical explanation for their inability to conceive a child. Concerned about the plight of these women, Bro. Ibe began to search the Scriptures for answers.

One attribute that everyone who knew Bro. Ibe ascribed to him was his heart of love and compassion. His love for people was deep and sincere. He would go to any length to meet the needs of others, especially spiritual needs. Where others would naturally stop caring, Bro. Ibe would continue reaching out in love. For instance, the story was told of a doctor, a colleague of

Bro. Ibe in Medical School, who got saved because of this virtue of genuine love, compassion and perseverance. This doctor sometimes came to the Christian fellowship smelling of cigarette and drink. He would sit at the back of the hall with a cigarette in his mouth. Virtually all the brethren made sure they kept comfortable distances away from him. But Bro. Ibe would always draw close and spend time talking with him. The doctor soon found Christ and became a useful instrument in the hands of God in UCH.[3]

Gbemi Olaleye was a student at the School of Nursing in UCH between 1981 and 1985. She became acquainted with Bro. Ibe through the UCH Christian Fellowship, and later joined the ministers at Faith Clinic when it eventually started. She remembers him as a man of "deep compassion and great love for people."[4]

The Scriptures reveal that the miraculous workings of God often manifested in and through the life of Christ because of the compassion that He had on the people.[5] Moved with the same kind of compassion, Bro. Ibe prayed earnestly for his patients in his closet. Before long, God began to open his eyes to truths in the word. He found that some of the conditions that people had in the days of Christ were caused by demonic oppression. When Jesus intervened on behalf of those who were thus afflicted, He did not just pray for their healing; He dealt with the root cause of their affliction. For instance, there were some deaf and dumb people that He simply healed,[6] and there were others that he had to cast out the deaf-and-dumb spirit before the healing manifested.

And he was casting out a devil, and it was dumb. And it came to pass, when the devil was gone out, the dumb spake; and the people wondered.[7]

Armed with this understanding, Bro. Ibe yielded to the prompting of the Holy Spirit to pray for clients whose cases were beyond medical reasoning. He obeyed God and began to invite them and their husbands to his house for prayer. Soon, results began to follow. After he cast out the spirits that manifested during prayer, the women who were once victims of serious gynaecological problems, found lasting solutions. Those who could not bear children began to conceive. As a result, many who did not yet know the Lord gave their hearts to Christ.

All that Bro. Ibe had done was follow the leading of God, address the spiritual root of the afflictions and take authority over any spirit that was responsible for them! Everything was done from a heart of compassion, a desire to be of help and a conviction that nothing is impossible for God. This was the beginning of a fresh ministerial journey Bro. Ibe would take alongside the One who had called him before the foundations of the earth.

RESOLVING THE WORK-MINISTRY CONFLICT

As a staff at UCH, Dr. Ibeneme was wholly dedicated to his job (as a matter of fact, he practiced medicine throughout the Faith Clinic years up to the time of his death). However, as an ambassador of heaven in that establishment, he was fully sold out to God's cause. The more he prayed for people, the more he saw results.

Those who had testimonies of miraculous turnarounds began to spread the word to others with similar issues. Before long, there was an increase in both medical and spiritual activity around the doctor's office.

Inevitably, the enemy who was afflicting these women and their families was not happy with Bro. Ibe because his works were being destroyed irreversibly through the prayers of God's servant. The only way the devil could try and deter him was to stir up opposition against him at work. Soon, both colleagues and the hospital management began to persecute Bro. Ibe. He was labelled a religious fanatic and warned about his "unofficial" activities that conflicted with his medical practice. But like the apostles of old, Bro. Ibe could not stop testifying about the mighty Deliverer who was the ultimate solution to his patients' tribulations. More and more people needed spiritual attention, and he was willing for God to use him to meet their needs.

The wisdom that God ministered to Bro. Ibe was to start inviting those with beyond-medical problems to his house for fellowship and prayer. He lived at the UCH residential quarters, in House 5 (simply called "House 5" by Faith Clinic ministers). This, then, was the beginning of the ministry. It was a convenient way to separate Bro. Ibe's day-to-day medical practice from his ever-increasing spiritual activities.

The truth is, Faith Clinic Nigeria Inc. was not initially conceived as a ministry organisation. It grew into one. Once asked how she and her late husband conceived the idea for Faith Clinic, Sis. Ego gave the following response:

We didn't start as a ministry. We were having a fellowship. There was the University of Ibadan fellowship and any time brethren gathered, we prayed and sometimes people manifested and they were prayed for. This continued when we crossed to the University College Hospital (UCH). My spouse was two years ahead of me in the medical school. As medical doctors and Christians, we normally held prayer meetings at Preventive and Social Medicine unit of the University College Hospital (UCH). We didn't take it as a special ministry. People came to the fellowship with needs and we went all out to minister to them. We didn't see it as a calling, but as a part of the ministration of Jesus Christ.[8]

"JUST BRING YOUR FAITH"

Even the name "Faith Clinic" was not preconceived. From every indication, it was an accidental naming. Dr. Ibeneme usually held an antenatal clinic on Wednesdays at UCH. When he began to invite people to his house for prayer on Saturdays, his work-free day, the women would ask him what they needed to bring (perhaps expecting a long list of spiritual items). Bro. Ibe would simply say, "Just bring your faith... and if you have a Bible, bring it as well."

The women then began to tell each other that they were going the doctor's "faith" clinic — since faith was all that they needed to bring to the "appointment." This is how the name "Faith Clinic" came about[9] (more like how the name "Christian" became the label for identifying the followers of Christ in Antioch[10]). Attendees were coming by faith to the clinic of Doctor Jesus for their long-standing yokes to be broken and their heavy burdens removed! Bro. Ibe believed literally that "without faith it was impossible to please God" and that all things were possible to him who believed in God.

Everyone who knew Bro. Ibe testified freely that he was highly anointed by God to minister deliverance to the captives. These beginnings give some insight into why this was the case. Bro. Ibe did not seek for the power of God for any personal reason; he did not venture out to build a ministry organisation; he simply made himself available to God for the deliverance others. He walked in selfless love and was readily moved by people's sufferings. God, therefore, noting the genuineness of his heart, anointed him with the Holy Ghost and power so he could minister effectively to the oppressed.

As Remi Tejumola, one of the former ministers and staff members at Faith Clinic, said: "We ministered by faith, but Bro. Ibeneme ministered with the revelational gifts of the Holy Spirit."[11] These gifts began to manifest as he prayed earnestly for his "clients." The more they came, the more the operation of the gifts grew in his life.

3

FROM HOUSE 5 TO
THE LECTURE THEATRE

News about what God was doing at the House 5 prayer meetings spread very quickly. The best form of publicity was in operation: word of mouth! People told people. Testimonies of deliverance multiplied from week to week.

The truth is, throughout the revival years, Faith Clinic never put up any formal advertisement. No flyer was printed; no radio announcement was made. The miracles of deliverance that were happening frequently in people's lives, types that were not being witnessed elsewhere, were attracting people to the prayer meetings.

The response of the people to this 'new phenomena' was similar to those who saw the authority of Christ over evil spirits:

> And they were all amazed, and spake among themselves, saying, What a word is this! For with authority and power he commandeth the unclean spirits,

and they come out. And the fame of him went out into every place of the country round about.[1]

Due to the growing number of people who attended the prayer meetings, Bro. Ibe had to move the fellowship out of House 5. He was able to secure the use of one of the lecture rooms in UCH – the Preventive and Social Medicine (PSM) unit lecture room. The people that came were just a handful at first, but it was not long before the hall was packed full.

The motivation for Faith Clinic was to help and minister to people through faith in the name of Jesus Christ. The underlying passion was to lead the unsaved to the cross for the salvation of their souls. However, the distinguishing mark of the ministry, that which made it stand apart from others, was the display of authority over the demonic realm. Every Saturday night at the PSM lecture theatre, the works of satan in the lives of people were being destroyed, and the sight of demons being cast out of the oppressed continued to amaze the believers.

Holding the all-night programme from Saturday evening to the early hours of Sunday morning worked for everyone. Bro. Ibe, as mentioned earlier, was a practising gynaecologist at the UCH; those who attended were also busy all week; ministering deliverance sometimes required adequate time for counselling and prayer; and most importantly, Faith Clinic was interdenominational because it drew people from every kind of church background. Attending Faith Clinic on a Saturday night, therefore, did not interfere with one's membership in a local church. On the contrary, God used Faith Clinic to add tremendous value, not only to the lives of those who attended, but also to the churches that they were affiliated to.

THE "ORDER OF SERVICE"

One unique feature of Faith Clinic from its inception was the manner in which the meetings were structured. It was an efficient order that did not stifle the move of the Spirit. Rather than hinder the Spirit, the service schedule aided it greatly.

Most people will remember Faith Clinic as a "deliverance ministry," the first of its kind in Nigeria. The reality was that so much more than deliverance happened at Faith Clinic every week. It was a hub of wide-ranging spiritual activities that consistently populated heaven and plundered hell. Deliverance was a part of what transpired – a major part indeed – but only a part of an integrated whole. What you witnessed consistently at Faith Clinic was the salvation of the lost, healing of the sick, baptism of believers in the Holy Spirit with the initial evidence of speaking in tongues, and, of course, deliverance of the oppressed from demonic bondage. It was a "full gospel" operation, perhaps stemming from Bro. Ibe's Pentecostal roots on campus as well as his involvement with the Full Gospel Business Men's movement. Later on, a Bible School was introduced to ground the believers in the faith. The all-night service was effectively ordered to accommodate all these aspects of ministry.

PRAISE AND WORSHIP

The programme usually started with a session of vibrant praise and worship. In the early days at the PSM lecture room, there were no musical instruments. The PA equipment was a simple radio-powered microphone. In spite of the absence of sophisticated gadgets, people sang praises to God and clapped their hands enthusiastically. Those who had tambourines brought them along. The absence of a keyboard or drum set was not a deterrent for the anointing.

During this time of unaccompanied worship, the presence of God was mightily felt. Quite often, demons would start to manifest through people because they could not stand the weight and intensity of God's glory!

I cannot forget some of the songs we sang in those days; simple songs that created a tangible and unmistakeable atmosphere of faith in the room:

There is power mighty in the blood

There is power mighty in the blood

There is power mighty in the blood of Jesus Christ

There is power mighty in the blood

Years later, when Faith Clinic moved to the much bigger Adamasingba stadium, there was space for musical instruments and skilful musicians. These, however, did not dilute the presence of God because the focus was always on Jesus – who He is and what faith in His name can do.

After the vibrant worship session, a pair of ministers (a main speaker and one interpreting into Yoruba, the main indigenous language in the Ibadan region) would come on stage to deliver a salvation message (usually called the "first message"). After this session, another pair of ministers took people's testimonies. Next, there was a healing message and prayers for healing. Then, the much anticipated "second message" that led to the ministry of deliverance. Finally, those who had gotten saved and delivered were exhorted about the Holy Spirit, and hands are laid on them for the baptism of the Holy Spirit. This arrangement worked seamlessly and it ensured that the night was fully optimised. There was hardly a dull moment at Faith Clinic because God was always at work round the clock!

THE "FIRST MESSAGE"

The need for and means of salvation were always explained from the Scriptures, followed by an altar call. Many had come because of one issue or the other, and it was expedient that they understood the prerequisite to deliverance, which was faith in the finished work of Christ's cross. There was no point casting a devil out of an unsaved person because the demon would easily gain access back into the person and the end of such would be worse than the beginning.[2]

Every week, scores of people gave their lives to Christ. It is not possible to quantify the number of people who became born again during the Faith Clinic years. Remi Tejumola revealed that they once decided to keep a tab on the number of conversions in one particular year. By the end of that year, about ten thousand people had responded to the call for salvation.[3] Besides, the conversions in those days were deep and genuine.

The following written testimonies of salvation were documented randomly by two people who had gotten saved through the influence of Faith Clinic. Both testimonies acknowledge the ministry of Bro. Ibeneme, and were posted on a website dedicated solely to salvation stories.[4] The first was posted by Deaconess Abigail Osunbunmi.

> I thank God for the salvation of my soul. What a story to tell all the days of my life. I was born into a Muslim family and was taught never to allow anybody to sweet-talk me into any religion. In this light, with an opportunity to effect changes as a prefect in secondary school, I convinced my fellow Muslims to rescind going to church. Then I convinced my principal to enforce Muslims to attend mosques on Fridays.
>
> Little did I know that I was hindering people from receiving salvation, [and was] keeping them away from embracing the love of God. I did these things ignorantly until I finished my secondary school education. I met with Christ two years after graduating from secondary school.
>
> As a student nurse, I had the opportunity to meet Dr. Ibeneme who told me about Jesus in the Doctor's Room Adeoyo Hospital Ibadan. The doctor invited me to a faith clinic in the chapel of Resurrection University of Ibadan where I gave my life to our lord Jesus in September 1981.[5] That night was an encounter with the Lord, one to remember.

I cried all night for my sin. It got to a point that the brethren had to leave me to cry until I was tired of crying. I was glad that somebody died for my sins and I felt the only thing to do for such a Person is to (1) never go back to the world, and (2) I wanted everybody to hear the story of my salvation and invite them to Christ. This was a concern to my family. They believed I had lost my mind. My mother was worried and started looking for help for me if perhaps I can change my mind, but rather I kept praying for all my family. God said He will save me and my entire household.

Alas, my mother eventually confessed the lordship of our Lord Jesus Christ at 93 years of age![6]

The second testimony of salvation was posted by Obasuyi Doris Nkem:

I got born again at the age of 10 through a family friend back in Ibadan, during a Faith Clinic with Rev. Ibeneme who is now late. I have since grown in the Lord and am so glad I made this decision because far back then, my family who are royal, were involved in a lot of sacrifices and oracles, but they have now accepted the light. Glory to God![7]

The current pastor of the Yoruba congregation of Stone Church in Mokola, Ibadan, Pastor Oluwole, gave his life to Christ during a Faith Clinic meeting in 1985. He went on to attend the Faith Clinic Bible School and is now being used of God to minister life to others.[8] Eternity will fully reveal the extent to which Bro. Ibe and the ministry of Faith Clinic were used of God to introduce people to Christ.

TESTIMONY TIME!

After the salvation message and an interlude of praise, another pair of ministers came up stage to take people's testimonies – and there was always a queue of people wanting to share what God had done in their lives. Deliverances, healings and diverse miracles were happening every week and there was never enough time to tell all that God had done. The testimony time was always one to look forward to. Not only did it encourage the faith of those who had come expecting a miracle from God, it also edified the conviction of believers that God was all-powerful and worthy of total consecration. There was no hype or fanfare in the Faith Clinic atmosphere; just the unshakeable awareness that God is real.

The faith-charged atmosphere of Faith Clinic drew people like a magnet. It was an atmosphere conducive for the salvation of sinners, deliverance of the oppressed and rapid spiritual growth of the believers. You always left Faith Clinic fully aware of the reality of God and a longing for a personal walk with Him. Although God used Bro. Ibeneme on numerous occasions, the focus was always on Jesus Christ the Healer and Deliverer.

The following testimony was documented by Lekan Obasuyi as part of an academic thesis about *"A New Genre of Autobiography in African Folklore."*[9] Although the testimony was given after the ministry had moved from the PSM lecture hall, it portrays vividly the Faith Clinic atmosphere, the manner in which the night-long programme was ordered and the impact that testimonies had in every programme. The writer, commenting on the

fact that the testifier, Sade Fadipe, was female, wrote the
following endnote:

> It is not only women who are prone to giving testi-
> monies, but at the start of the Christian revival, there
> were more women involved than men. I am
> currently working on two testimonies, one of them
> by a former prophet of the Aladura church. *This
> prophet reluctantly accepted an invitation to the Faith
> Clinic, Ibadan. As it turned out, the prophet attended on
> the day Sade was to give her testimony. At the end of
> Sade's testimony, the prophet gave his life to Christ* and
> shortly thereafter was a guest speaker at the same
> venue.[10] (*emphasis mine*).

Here is the testimony restated in full as documented in
this account:

> Sade's testimony – her real first name is Sade – was
> given live in 1989 at an open-air night vigil organ-
> ised by the Faith Clinic mission founded by Dr. E
> (sic) Ibeneme, a Christian medical practitioner with
> the University College Hospital, Ibadan. The venue
> was the Adekunle Fajuyi sporting complex,[11]
> Ibadan, Nigeria. On a slightly chilly night – and you
> can tell from the way the large audience is rigged
> out in warm clothing – Sade is called out to the
> podium and Christian choruses rendered to the
> accompaniment of a live Christian band that has
> been invited to the occasion. The band is led by a
> woman – the lead singer – who sings and dances
> and empathises with the audience who join in with
> the singing and clapping and dancing. On the small-

ish podium that faces the covered stands where the audience is gathered, there are two microphones, a wooden lectern, and a female interpreter, apart from Sade herself. On the ground near the raised plat-form on which Sade and the interpreter are standing is a heap of assorted items – rather unusual personal effects – which turn out to be those of Sade and in time become crucial to the narrative.

There are strong beams of tractable light, some of which serve the video camera brought in to cover the proceedings. Behind Sade and the interpreter is a wire fence that separates the outside world from the momentous event taking place within. Sade is introduced to the audience and it is immediately clear that the venue scores rather low acoustically. The open air above the podium throws away the sounds from the loudspeakers in a wanton disper-sal. But this is made up for by the confident and inspired delivery of the celebrant.

Sade takes the microphone and explains her deci-sion to speak in her native Yoruba in terms of her being more comfortable and competent in this language. The bilingual interpreter repeats in reasonably good English what Sade has said, rather less than accurately. The advantage in devoting greater attention to the Yoruba original is soon enough clear to the bilingual listener.

Sade was born in 1956 to caring loving parents who are nominal Christians. She grows up in a rather carefree happy-go-lucky atmosphere. She goes through elementary school and high school like any normal child. After high school, she contemplates a future of further studies but meanwhile becomes seriously involved with a young man, and before long they are married. Her wedding is the "high-society" type involving a lot of noise, wining, dining, and publicity in some Nigerian newspapers.

She is married and expects quite naturally to have a baby within the first year of her marriage. Among the Yoruba, the success of a marriage is measured more in terms of fertility than by the childless felicity of the couple. The first few years of her marriage indicate that there is a problem. She and her husband decide at some point that it might be wise for her to see a doctor on the issue. She consults a number of reputable gynaecologists on the matter but all they do is reassure her that things will be all right and advise that she should take things easy, as it is not uncommon for newly married couples to fail to have a child during the first few years of their marriage. She believes the doctors and decides to give some attention to her professional career in the interim. With her husband's permission, she proceeds to the United Kingdom on a short course in Home Economics. While there, she takes the opportunity to visit specialists in obstetrics and gynaecology. It is at this point that a series of medical tests reveal she does not have Fallopian tubes; that she had been born without these tubes which are vital to female reproductivity (sic). The doctors are amazed as she.

She is given a pile of X-ray films which show the absence of the F-tubes in her.

Sade breaks into a Christian chorus at this point, and dancing and describing God as a miracle-working God, she lifts up from the lectern a few X-ray films of her body. She explains that there had been a huge pile of these X-ray films but that she has given many of them away to curious Nigerian doctors and medical students. She tells members of the audience that they are welcome to the remainder of the films for inspection any day. Both the ironic ring of the lyric she is singing and the timeliness of the action – the presentation of the X-ray films – have the effect of leaving the audience spellbound and curious. The arena falls silent as Sade pauses for breath. The video cameraman loses himself completely, forgetting for a while that the camera he is carrying is supposed to see what he himself is seeing. Rather, the camera falls out of focus, staring balefully at some insignificant part of the arena while the man's eyes are riveted on the testifier. This happens rather frequently and subsequently spoils the fun for those who hear Sade on cellulose.

At the end of her course in Britain, Sade returns to her husband in Nigeria and lies to him about the true condition, fearful that should he learn the truth, he could put her away and marry another woman. She tells him the British experts have assured that she has the capacity to have as many children as she wants. Her husband believes her; still, she weeps in secret any time she remembers the truth about her condition. She encounters greater difficulty with her husband's relations on the issue of her childlessness. As the years pass by and she has not had even a miscarriage to prove her ability to become pregnant, her in-laws become more unreasonable and begins to visit *babalawos,* sorcerers, in Nigeria, Niger Republic, and Ivory Coast. An old woman on the same street in the big Yoruba town where she is living at this time calls her one day and tells her she has learnt from reliable sources about her childlessness. The crone announces that her problem is actually quite soluble. Sade asks her how, and she says it can only be done on condition that Sade is initiated into witchcraft. On an appointed night, Sade joins a coven for the initiation rites during which the witches ask for a part of her flesh and blood. She allows them to cut into her buttocks – which still bear the scars of initiation. She is soon able to fly about at night to attend meetings, physically disembodied. She acquires skills in witchcraft, sorcery, and necromancy quite quickly and comes to be respected and feared in the world of witches. She discovers and revels in the fact that the whole point about witchcraft is inexplicable hatred towards ordinary people and vengeance for real and imagined offences, in regard to which the witch can bring on the plagues or kill, using diabolical methods. As a witch, she has needlessly ruined hundreds of lives before the crone who brought her into witchcraft confesses to her that if she is not naturally equipped to have a baby in the first place, the best (or worst?) of witches can do nothing about it. She adds that having babies is actually contrary to the aim of witchcraft; preventing those who can from having babies is a far more fulfilling option for a witch.

Beckoning to the ushers, Sade begins to receive on the podium some of the personal effects heaped on the ground near her. She holds up a magic skirt and explains that it is perhaps the most potent of the magic accoutrements in a witch's wardrobe. She lifts up a magic earthen pot and a blood-sucking girdle and explains that the magic girdle is used to drain a victim's blood, which is then stored up in the medium -sized pot that can hold, uncannily, several hundreds of litres of human blood. The blood itself is drunk by the witches at the Sabbaths. Sade begins to sing: "There is power mighty in the blood of Jesus Christ..." The audience, as one person, snaps out of petrifaction. Led by Sade on the podium, there is more singing and dancing. She displays many other items of witchcraft and sorcery and continues her story.

Disappointed at the crone's duplicity, she continues to attend the Sabbaths and wreaks even greater havoc among ordinary folk who have offended her or been reported to her for punishment by her mates in the sisterhood. She has now attained a high degree of callousness and sadism, deriving kicks from acts of unspeakable wickedness and hatred. She remains completely dedicated to evil. She explains that the attitude of witches to church and church-goers is governed by sheer animus. Witches loathe Christians. She tells about a mission she is given on one occasion by a more senior witch in her coven. A well-known evangelist – an armed robber before his Christian conversion and now a crowd-pulling man-of-God – named Kayode Williams is in town for a week-long open-air crusade (it is a big Yoruba town) and, as usual, it is expected that masses of people will attend his crusade. Sade is commissioned to disrupt the crusade by using all the diabolical means at her disposal. She takes off for the crusade grounds with rain-making charms since this was an open-air programme. She causes a deluge over the arena where the crusade is taking place and watches with glee as the evangelist is soaked with rain water where he is speaking from a raised platform and the downpour is such that he has difficulty retaining the attention of the large crowd of mostly youths. Her aim is to spoil the show for him by precipitating heavy rainfall on each of the scheduled seven days of the crusade. However, on the third day of the crusade as the evangelist is about to deliver his Christian message of the day amid another threatening thunderstorm, he looks around at the large crowd that milled about him and declares that some evildoers are about who are intent on disrupting his programme; that on the third day of their effort he is giving them the final chance to stop their evil ways and repent or face the consequence; that the God whom he serves is a merciful God, otherwise he, Mr. Williams, could command the earth to open up and swallow up those evildoers hiding in the crowd whose aim is to cause mayhem where there should be peace; that the aim of the crusade is to bring about the reconciliation of the sinner to God through Jesus Christ. Hearing this, she is persuaded that the speaker must have at his behest greater powers than any witch can have at her command. So she flees the crusade grounds, and the crusade continues in excellent weather.

It is at this point that she becomes a high flier in her church, the type described as a "white garment church," whose founder is said to have received his inspiration and supernatural powers from a bird, a snake, and a monkey in the thick of an African forest, and whose members pad barefoot about the church premises. In practice, this church mixes biblical precepts with indigenous rites, encouraging its members to indulge in spiritual syncretism themselves. Its leadership, she says, is raised on the stilts of deception, duplicity, and fraud, while the laity are nurtured on lies, deceit, and self-delusion. She is a high-flying leader at this church because of her magical skills, which she presses into service in the church, and, as a result, she is described as an accomplished seer and prophetess. She sometimes flies bird-like to church service right from the witches' Sabbaths. On one occasion, another great seer and prophetess like herself at the same church discloses to her in a private power struggle between them that her own brand of occult power is superior to that of a witch and Sade is left in a fit of pique.

Spellbound, the audience watch or join in on the intermittent Christian chorus renditions led by Sade, who begins to show off one after another some of the garments of her high office as a church leader. Apart from the robes, there is an assortment of crosses and other items of satanic worship, including candles, incense, perfumes, a special kind of water which is called "green water," drawn from seven rivers, and which is widely believed to be magical. Despite her achievements as a witch and prophetess, she still feels unfulfilled and yearns for a child, her own, to hold and to cuddle. Deep down in her heart, she knows it is a hopeless cause, a futile desire, as there is no biological basis for her kind of expectation.

She is surprised one day when a young woman and a man approach her at her house declaring that they have come to preach the gospel to her. She cannot hide her annoyance at the announcement. It is raining outside, so she plants herself squarely at the doorway such that the strangers cannot get into the house, and she tells them she is listening. The two evangelists stand meekly in the heavy rain and begin eagerly to talk. She listens to them patiently as they talk to her about Jesus Christ and how he came because of sinners; how the supreme sacrifice he has paid for the sinner is as relevant and valid today as it was two thousand years ago; how this has come to be because of God's love for us. They conclude that a sinner's ultimate destination is hell. Sade smiles with satisfaction as she contemplates the speakers.

She smiles not so much because of the points they are busy trying to make – none of it makes any sense to her – but because she can see that they have become thoroughly drenched with rain water and do not appear to mind. At length, the evangelists go away promising they will call again. They do so before the week has run out and thereafter continue to visit her regularly to her utter irritation. One day they invite her to their fellowship and she follows them, surprised at herself.

At the Christian fellowship, they sing and clap and there are prayer requests. The meeting goes into a session of prayers, during which the fellowship leader prays for her. As the prayers are being said all around, she falls into a state of trance and has a vision. In the vision, a tall fair-looking person in white comes over to her and performs some surgical work on her. He separates her body into two length-wise, that is, from head downward, and implants something in her midriff. He brings her members back together again and then disappears. Sade gets pregnant within one month of this experience. Elated, she stops attending the Christian fellowship and returns to the witches' coven. But she carries the pregnancy for over two years, unable to give birth. She soon realises that she is under a magic spell. She tries all kinds of sorcery and witchcraft to remove the magic ban but fails. She is eventually persuaded to return to the Christian fellowship. *There they pray for her and send her to Dr. Ibeneme's Faith Clinic, where she is successfully delivered of a baby girl and gives her life to Christ.* The audience responds with applause and bursts into songs of praise to God, dancing, as an usher hands Sade her little girl on the podium.[12] (*emphasis mine*).

These kinds of testimonies that highlighted God's might and goodness abounded at Faith Clinic and they were a vital part of the night's programme. Some were simple and short; others were detailed and long; but all were to the glory of God. After hearing a testimony like Sade's, the faith of many who had come seeking God for one thing or the other comes to life. Those who were not yet converted, like the Aladura prophet who heard Sade's testimony, made up their minds to receive Christ into their lives.

Above all, the name of Jesus is lifted high and glory is given to God for the display of His power. Everyone at Faith Clinic believed and walked in the truth of the Scripture that said, "They overcame him (the great dragon) by the blood of the Lamb, and by the word of their testimony."[13]

4

MANIFESTATIONS OF POWER!

After the testimony time, another pair of ministers came up stage for the healing message and ministry. Understandably, most people remember Faith Clinic for deliverance, but so much happened during the healing session. Cancers got healed. Ulcers disappeared. Deaf ears opened. All manners of miracles happened to the glory of God.

Remi Tejumola, in a blog post, wrote about an experience he had while conducting one of the healing sessions:

> One night, during the all-night meeting at the Faith Clinic, I took the Healing Session and preached on "Casting Your Cares Upon the Lord," which is based on 1 Peter 5:7. As I led the people in prayer, my interpreter's eyes got opened into the spirit realm, and she saw that an angel of God rushed in with a basket into the auditorium collecting all the cares of the people who believed, and many people got healed that night![1]

The gifts of the spirit operated freely during this time — gifts of healing, word of knowledge, miracles etc. While the wonder of expelling demons was a primary talking point among those who attended Faith Clinic, the healing testimonies were equally compelling. They happened as frequently as the deliverance ministrations. The same God was at work among the people, manifesting His glory and power. The healings that occurred convinced many that God was real. They also raised the level of their expectation for deliverance.

"SECOND MESSAGE"

The message that led to the deliverance sessions, called the "second message," was always after the healing message on the "order of service." By this time, you could literally feel the power of God in the air. The expectation of those seeking a touch from God was high. The cynicism of those who came with a critical mind (and there were always some in that category) had no impact whatsoever on the atmosphere. More often than not, such people left with a change of heart.

This was the session that many people had heard about and looked forward to, especially those who had come for the first time. The power of God over evil spirits would soon be demonstrated in a visible way. If the testimonies about what God had done in the lives of others were astounding, the live manifestations of the power of God over the devil were even more fascinating. The Bible was going to come alive in the presence of everyone. Jesus had said that people would not believe until they see the miraculous power of God,[2] and that is exactly what you saw when you attended Faith Clinic.

In the early days at the PSM lecture hall, the exhortation that led to the deliverance session was often taken by Bro. Ibeneme. As the number of ministers increased, and as Bro. Ibeneme began to travel for outside ministrations, others took turns to lead this session.

Bro. Ibe was highly anointed by God for the ministry of deliverance. His presence alone, it seemed, had a torturing effect on demons. As we noted earlier, this grace did not come on him overnight. God considered him faithful and entrusted him with unction for the demonstration of the believer's authority. He was confident in God and fearless before the devil. With great conviction, he would tell the expectant crowd that Jesus will meet them at the point of their needs – no matter the need. And there was much need in the lives of people.

Many issues that people were facing defied explanation. Just like the woman with the issue of blood who received her healing when she touched the hem of Christ's garment, many had exhausted their resources and spent much time looking for solutions to their predicaments.[3] Many of the unsaved, prior to visiting Faith Clinic, had frequented herbalists and "white garment" prayer houses without any solution to their problems. Those who were already believers had prayed for years and at times, yielded to the temptation to seek help from "special prophets." Faith Clinic, for quite a number, was the last resort. Thank God they were never disappointed. Just as Jesus had said, "Come unto me all ye that labour and are heavily laden, and I will give you rest,"[4] people came burdened to Faith Clinic, but went back home totally free!

The issues that people came with were also diverse. There was no shortage of those who had difficulties conceiving a child – the major condition that led to the founding of Faith Clinic. Others had chronic illnesses that medicine could not correct. There were those who consistently experienced spiritual oppression in dreams and in real life. The spiritual growth of others was stunted for years irrespective of their efforts to walk with God. No matter the nature of the problem, there was a common underlying cause – the evil activity of demons, and either the people's ignorance about it or inability to do anything about it.

God gave Bro. Ibe much insight into the nature of these activities and faith in the power of God over the evil entities. God used him to teach strongly on the power of the cross of Christ that nullifies generational curses, overcomes demonic oppression or possession, defeats household wickedness and removes any legal ground for demonic activity.[5] People were facing long-standing, unexplainable challenges that threatened their very existence and they did not need mere theoretical postulations and lengthy rituals; what they required was a practical demonstration of the love and power of God, which is exactly what the deliverance sessions were all about.

DELIVERANCE SESSIONS

Simply, the manifestation of power at the meetings was awesome. Similar to what Jesus experienced when He ministered in the synagogues, it was common for demons to start screaming when Bro. Ibe begins his exhortation. When this happened, the ministers will take the persons outside and start ministering to them. There have been times when Bro. Ibe would walk through the aisle or stand in front of a person to be prayed for, and demons would begin to manifest. Stern commands in the name of Jesus – "come out of him in Jesus' name!" – got demons crying out in panic.

Whether it was Bro. Ibe or another minister taking the pre-deliverance exhortation and prayer, it was always amazing to see the ministers "raking" demons from the crowd. ("Raking" was the term some ministers used to refer to the collective rebuking of demons, which usually resulted in some people manifesting). You were always left with no iota of doubt that every knee bows at the mention of the name of Jesus. Your faith in God and His word is built up and your authority in Christ affirmed.

The deliverance ministration itself was usually simple: demonic entities were ordered out of people in the name of Jesus. However, the departure of the evil spirits from people was, a lot of the time, dramatic; it was usually accompanied by people throwing up (vomiting), scream-ing, yawning or manifesting in some other visible way. Sometimes, it took a while before a person was 'totally delivered,' and at other times, the process was very short. No matter the length of time required, the ministers were always patient. All the sessions were conducted in the open, with the ministers ministering together as a team, usually in pairs.

Some of the sessions were quite unusual. Bro. Ibe was once ministering to a lady who had difficulties conceiving a child. As the demons were leaving, the woman was vomiting mucus. Bro. Ibe and those ministering with him noticed an office pin in the woman's vomit. Concluding that it must be from the notice board that was hanging close to where they were ministering, they moved the woman to another location. Just then, she vomited again and another office pin was found in her mucus. Suddenly, the woman reached for the pin and wanted to swallow it. The ministers held her hand and commanded the demons to leave without any further delay. They did and the woman was completely delivered. Subsequently, she was able to conceive and give birth to a child. Evidently, the pins were used to block her fallopian tubes in the spirit realm, preventing her from having a baby.[6]

Remi Tejumola narrated an experience in a blog post:

> One day while ministering deliverance to a man at the Faith Clinic, the demon in him spoke up and said, "God has been trying to bless this man, but we've been hindering him from receiving." I just said, "Therefore, I open the windows of heaven and take a bucket of blessings, and pour it now on him" (actually demonstrating what I said as if I was carrying a real bucket and pouring it on him) and the man shook from head to his toes as he got delivered through that act of faith.[7]

A lady was brought from Ijebu-Ode in a very terrible state. She was held in chains because of her mental instability, and had to be restrained throughout the meeting. After the deliverance session early in the morning, she got up from the floor fully in her right mind. She asked the people around where she was and how she got there. When she was told how she had disrupted the meeting all night, she almost went to all the ministers to apologise for her behaviour. Everyone praised God for her deliverance. It was days later, however, that her full story came to light.

Her father travelled all the way from Ijebu-Ode to give the testimony to Bro. Ibe. Eight years to this time, his daughter came home from the United States with her fiancé to get married in Nigeria. She brought all her clothing for the wedding from USA, and gave them to her father to keep until the wedding day. He had kept them securely in a cupboard in his room. Two days to the traditional wedding, he needed to take something from the cupboard and to his surprise, could not find any of the wedding items. They had completely vanished! No one in the house had gone into cupboard or could explain how the items had gotten lost.

Needing to carry on with the ceremony, the woman hurried to buy a new wedding dress and every other item that she needed for the occasion. On getting back to America, the new couple began to have serious problems. The issues got so severe that the husband, who could not take them any longer, divorced her. This was what led to her losing her mind. She was flown back to Nigeria and had been a lunatic until her glorious deliverance at Faith Clinic.

The reason why the father came back in search of Bro. Ibe was the astonishing thing that happened after they returned to Ijebu-Ode from Faith Clinic. Someone had gone to the cupboard to take something only to find all the items that had vanished eight years ago in the same place that they were before they disappeared! The devil had returned the things he had stolen from her. The man did not have any hesitation receiving Christ as His Lord and Saviour.[8]

THE DELIVERANCE OF AUNTY CHRISTIE

The deliverance of Aunty Christie, documented in her book titled *Alive at Last: A personal story of deliverance from the bondage of evil*,[9] is a testimonial to the awesomeness of God's power. It portrays the kind of burden people bore and gives some insight into the simplicity and effectiveness of the deliverance ministrations at Faith Clinic.

Bro. Ibeneme wrote the following foreword to *Alive at Last* (and being the only writing of his that I have found, I hereby present it in full):

> I first met Mrs. Ifebueme on that fateful night at a Full Gospel Business Men's outreach at the Premier Hotel Ibadan, when she met with the Lord Jesus Christ who changed her life and completely delivered her from the kingdom of darkness. That night, I was called to see this nicely dressed Igbo woman who had all her dresses completely soaked with tears and was asking

for me – yet, I had never met her before. However, I calmed her down and was then able to counsel with her, assuring her that the Lord has accepted her and was going to deliver her completely. This is therefore her story as was told by herself.

This story usually sends out chills and mixed feelings to the hearers each time she gave her testimony. This was expressed in the words of our dear sister, Miss Dupe Ogunbiyi who edited all the manuscripts of this book. I quote: "I was dumbfounded. It all seemed quite unreal and I wondered how such a vivacious looking young woman could have been through so much. The reality of my own happy state in the Lord Jesus Christ was brought to me anew." I wonder what your own experience would be but be it as it may, this story clearly shows that Jesus is Lord indeed.

Many years have passed since those tragedies took place in the life of our sister, and it has taken the special grace of God for her to relive this experience. It has taken much courage to put down on paper many of the facts that were best forgotten. However, this lady has never looked back since the day she was saved and has now become a terror to the camp of the devil. God has been using her to lead many others to Christ and assisting in their deliverances from the powers of darkness.

I wish you a pleasant and inspiring time of reading. It is my prayer that if you are not yet born-again, this book might make it plain to you. If also you find yourself in a situation as this, be assured that the Lord Jesus Christ is also able to set you free and you shall be free indeed.

> **Dr. I.K.U. Ibeneme**
> **President/Founder**
> **Faith Clinic Nigeria**[10]

Aunty Christie acknowledged the significant role Bro. Ibe played in her life and in the writing of the book:

> I must mention specifically Dr. I.K.U. Ibeneme of the Faith Clinic, Ibadan, whom I now consider a member of my earthly family and more importantly, a brother in the Lord Jesus Christ. He has invited me to give my testimony at various places all over the country and I thank God that through this testimony, many have come to know the salvation that is in Christ. He encouraged me to write this book and I can only pray for the great anointing of the Lord Jesus Christ in his life and work.[11]

Christiana Ifebueme was born on 6 June 1944 as the first child of Mr. Beniah Okoro and Mrs. Clarice Okoro. However, many years before her birth, her parents, Mr. & Mrs. Okoro, faced the possibility of a childless marriage. Every attempt to get pregnant failed. Every possible solution from a medical point of view was tried but they all proved futile. The only other solution, it seemed, was to seek help from traditional medicine.

This is exactly what Mrs. Okoro did. She began to go from one herbal healing home to another in search of a child. She was desperate for the shame of childlessness to be a thing of the past in her life.

Eventually, Mrs. Okoro "fell into the hands of a well-known local herbalist called *Baba*," who informed her that she was being influenced by "water spirits." Baba prescribed some sacrifices necessary to appease the spirits, to be carried out by the Aba waterside.

Not too long after Mrs. Okoro made the sacrifices and prayers were offered on her behalf, she became pregnant and gave birth to a baby girl. They called her Christiana. Other children followed in quick succession: a set of twins, Grace and Michael, then Henry, Edna, Janet, Promise and Cyprian. Before the encounter with Baba, they had no children; but now they had eight bundles of joy! What they were not aware of was that the devil never gives anything without strings attached to them. The blessings of parenthood came with much sorrow of heart.

When Henry, the child born after the twins, was still young, he began to have some strange experiences. He would suddenly start to scream and shout as if he was being chased by something. Afterwards, he would develop a very high fever. On one of these occasions, he began to convulse and later died. This was very heartbreaking, especially for Mrs. Okoro, but it was only the beginning of woes. Over a number of years, three more children (Michael, Cyprian and Promise) died from mysterious circumstances. Mr. Okoro also became a victim of this curse of death from the water spirits.

Christiana grew up in the midst of constant heartache. However, unknown to those around her, she was having problems of her own. As a young girl, she often had mysterious spiritual experiences that sometimes left her baffled. For instance, whenever she was by a bush, she seemed to hear the plants talking and understand what the birds were saying to each other. It seemed both strange and funny to her young mind. This experience was more intense whenever she went to the stream with other children. Instead of a serene atmosphere, the noise and disturbances were almost deafening. These were just a few of her troubles. The young Christiana had a catalogue of juvenile problems – academic, medical, behavioural and most of all, spiritual. She also developed a range of mystical abilities, like possessing intuitive knowledge about events before they happened (particularly when someone was going to die), having scary dreams and seeing strange beings around her all the time.

All these notwithstanding and against many odds, she eventually made it through Nursing School and got married to Samuel Ifebueme. Her new marital status ushered in a new level of spiritual attacks. She suddenly lost interest in her husband; her in-laws became antagonistic towards her; the fortune of her husband suddenly took a downward turn; her health issues worsened; her dreams about controlling entities intensified; and the lives of her five children were constantly at risk. All these complicated issues resulted in an endless search for freedom.

Christiana went from one herbalist to another; from one prayer house to another, all to no avail. They 'diagnosed' correctly that she was under the influence of water spirits, but their numerous prescriptions did nothing to alleviate the situation. Instead, she became increasingly impoverished by the unending list of items she needed to purchase her liberty.

Tired and exhausted, Christiana had gotten to the end of the road. The water spirits constantly threatened her life and that of her children and husband. Increasingly suicidal and understandably sceptical of anyone who offered to help, she did not know where to turn. Well, unknown to her, God was mindful of her situation and was about to reveal His love to her.

A friend invited Christiana to a dinner event organised by a group she had no knowledge about. It was a meeting of the Full Gospel Business Men's Fellowship in Ibadan. The only reason why she attended was the food and refreshments – and that aspect of the programme lived up to her expectations. After packing some food for her children at home, she was about to leave when an usher compelled her to stay for the rest of the meeting. She complied.

The rest of the programme featured a testimony by Evangelist Kayode Williams, an ex-armed robber who had turned to Christ. Christiana was amazed at how he could confidently talk about his past life and the change he had experienced. A second testimony was given by someone she knew and respected, Dr. Bolodeoku of the Department of Pathology, UCH. He narrated how he visited many 'white-garment' churches in search of rest from life's problems but only found peace when he encountered Jesus Christ. His story had a familiar tone to hers, and being someone she respected, it was not a struggle for her to respond positively to the altar call.

This was the beginning of her deliverance.

The series of events that happened next not only show the love and sovereignty of God, but also the role that Dr. Ibeneme and Faith Clinic played in the operations of God in those days.

After she prayed the sinner's prayer, another call was made for those who desired to receive the baptism of the Holy Spirit. Even though she did not know what it meant, she was curious enough to stay behind for prayer. Here's the rest of the story in Christiana's words:

> As soon as one of the men in charge laid his hand on me, my tongue started twisting and I heard myself saying things I could not understand. I tried to cover my mouth and stop saying the strange things but it did not work. All of my body was suddenly over-taken by a surging fire that I could not understand and almost immediately, I lost all consciousness.
>
> While unconscious, I saw myself on a big road, weeping and running blindly along, not knowing exactly where I was going. As I went along, I was desperately calling out to Jesus to help me; I was complaining that I had suffered so much in my life. Suddenly, a very huge man in an immaculate white garment stretched out his hands and held me saying:
>
> *My daughter, this is the end of your problems. Go to Dr. Ibeneme. He will help you and tell you what to do.*
>
> When I came back to myself and opened my eyes, I thought I had been there for only a few minutes,

but in fact I had been unconscious for almost two-and-a-half hours! Most of the people who attended the dinner had already left the hall. As I opened my eyes, I began to weep, calling desperately for Dr. Ibeneme. I kept shouting, *"Dr. Ibeneme, the Lord said I should come to you!"*

I could not stop myself from crying; neither did I know if Dr. Ibeneme was a man or a woman. I also did not know if he or she was present in the hall. I could not open my eyes properly because it was heavy with weeping.[12]

Thankfully, Dr. Ibeneme was in the building and some brethren took Christiana to him. She was still crying uncontrollably and it took a while for her to calm down. All she could do was show Dr. Ibeneme the long list of items she needed to buy for her next ritual in the "white garment" church. The doctor smiled and assured her that nothing was too big for the Lord. He invited her to Faith Clinic the following Saturday and asked her to bring all her children. Christiana recalls her initial reaction to the invitation:

I was quick to ask what I should bring along with me; what kind of jug I should use to draw water; how many days I should fast and what other items I should buy... The doctor told me that I did not have to come with anything. He told me to bring a sincere desire to know the Lord Jesus as Deliverer and all my agonies would become a thing of the past. If any fasting was at all necessary, he would be the one to undertake it rather than myself. And to crown it all,

I was not even going to pay him anything to do the fasting. It was all so straightforward and almost too easy for me to think it would work out in the end.[13]

Not only did it work out, the manner in which the Lord delivered Christiana reveals the supremacy of God's power as well as the simplicity of His operations in Faith Clinic. The rest of the story is best told in Christiana's words:

The one week of waiting before attending the Faith Clinic turned out to be a most agonising period for me. All the water demons could foresee what was about to happen and they intensified their pressure to make me change my mind about going to the Faith Clinic... They warned that if I dared to go to the Faith Clinic, they would end up killing me. They referred to the Christians as the 'Jesus People,' and told me that they would take away my power and stop me from seeing all those things I used to see concerning the future... Fortunately, the one week finally passed and Saturday night arrived... I took my five children along with me to the Faith Clinic... As soon as we arrived at the Faith Clinic, we were shown into a hall where people had already gathered, singing and praising God. There were few of them, about twenty people, to be attended to by the sisters and brothers at the clinic. They asked me to join in the singing but I was rather more interested in searching for Dr. Ibeneme who had invited me to the place. I was most disappointed when I was told he had travelled out of Ibadan. The Christians at the clinic then took time to explain to me that Dr. Ibeneme was not the one who would carry out the deliverance but the Lord Jesus Christ Himself. They encouraged me to believe in the Lord Jesus Christ with all my heart, soul and body, saying that I would surely be totally delivered. They explained that Dr. Ibeneme was a vessel whom God was using to solve many of our problems and that whether or not he was actually there, the faith I had brought with me would certainly get me my deliverance.

So my children and I joined in with the rest of the people and started singing and clapping to the choruses. A man later came up and preached such a beautiful and moving sermon, which again reduced me to tears. He made the message of salvation so clear that I was again overwhelmed by my errors of the past. All the while I had been frequenting the spiritual churches thinking that I knew Jesus Christ; I did not know that I was still very far from the truth.

Around midnight, the actual deliverance started. I thought I would see through it all but my power refused to work. Everything was blank to my mind. As I looked at the Christians, I saw a glowing fire protecting each of them and the blood of Jesus was clearly marked on them. It seemed as if nothing could attack them! When it was my turn to go for deliverance, I made up my mind that no one would humiliate me and braced myself to fight back in the event of any attack. I had come for deliverance and had waited anxiously for it, yet my inner mind kept warning me not to allow them to carry out the deliverance!

The most annoying aspect of everything that night was that instead of Dr. Ibeneme whom I had expected to see, a young boy, who was an undergraduate studying Petroleum Engineering at the University of Ibadan, was the one sent to minister to me. I thought it was simply ridiculous. What kind of power could such a young boy possess that would set me free from all my problems. Anyway, I would wait and see how far he could go. As the young man held my two hands, he made an accurate and startling statement of fact, yet he seemed so calm, confident and unperturbed. He spoke plainly, saying:

This is a water demon and queen of the sea.

I immediately started to wonder how he could so easily say what was wrong and in such a simple and straightforward manner! He wore ordinary clothes, had no flowing white or red robe; there were no candles or incense burning around him... yet the young man had hit the most crucial aspect of my situation so effortlessly! I was amazed.

The young man now proceeded with the actual deliverance.

In the name of Jesus, every knee shall bow. I command you water spirit to bow for Jesus and I command all contrary spirits to leave in Jesus' name.

As soon as he said this, I lost control of my legs and fell down... my whole body was on fire and I soon started to vomit. I had no control whatsoever over my actions. I must have fallen into a trance or had a broad daylight vision because I suddenly saw myself in a house under the sea, and I readily recognised it as the house in which I used to live as a sea queen. I saw the maids and male servants dashing about to see if they could lay their hands on valuable items to take with them. They had been caught totally unawares and the whole house was suddenly in total disarray. The maids would pick up an item, but as soon as the young man shouted, "Come out and go the Sahara Desert," they would immediately drop the item in sheer panic and run out of the house. My spiritual husband and all the children ran out in sheer panic. The man of the house was tying only a wrapper while the children held a mat over their heads as they ran crying towards the Sahara Desert.

All of a sudden, the big man realised that he was only tying a wrapper and that he was about to be displaced from his home. He boldly returned. I was undergoing an intermittent state of consciousness and unconsciousness so I could witness events in both worlds at the same time. The young man ministering to me asked me my name and I answered confidently that my name was "Jamuja." I tried to give the right answer, which was Christiana, but a loud masculine voice came forth telling them that my name was Jamuja. I could not control what I was saying and the next minute I was screaming:

Leave my wife alone! She is my wife! I want her! You have sent my children, servants and maids away. Leave my wife for me!

At this point, the Christians in the Faith Clinic began talking directly to the spirit that had been answering through me. They said:

Two thousand years ago, Jesus paid the price on the cross of Calvary, shedding His precious blood to set me free from death and bondage; and He made an open show of satan that anyone who believes in Him shall have life and everlasting peace.

They also went on to quote from the gospel according to John:

The thief cometh not but for the steal, and to kill and to destroy; I am come that they might have life and that they might have it more abundantly.

They went on to say that my body had become the temple of the living God and consequently, anything not planted there by God would be uprooted. As soon as they made this last statement, I screamed and started vomiting some more and suddenly I recollected myself. They now asked me my name and this time, I told them I was Christiana. At this, they all shouted 'Hallelujah!'[14]

Christiana and her children were soundly delivered that night by the touch of God and the power of the Word. She also experienced a fresh infilling of the Holy Spirit. Her husband, who was out of the country at the time, also received Christ upon his return. Dr. Ibeneme encouraged her to stand firm in the faith through prayer and studying the Bible. She later, by the Lord's direction, became an active member of the team of Faith Clinic ministers, where she would fondly be called Aunty Christie. Her testimony also touched many people across the country, especially during Full Gospel Business Men's events. She has been used of God to set many people free from the bondage of wicked spirits.

Jesus Christ is indeed the true Deliverer! How glorious it is when His mighty power to save and deliver is displayed through those who believe!

FILLED WITH THE SPIRIT!

The Faith Clinic programme always ended with a session on the baptism of the Holy Spirit. This practice traces the roots of the Faith Clinic revival to Pentecostalism, and places it on a par with the Azusa Street revival. The baptism of the Holy Spirit was as important as the deliverance session, if not more. After people were emptied of evil spirits, they needed to be filled with the Holy Spirit!

Around the early hours of the morning (about 4am or 5am), a final pair of ministers would exhort the tired but hungry believers about the importance of the Holy Spirit and what they should expect when hands are laid on them. Afterwards, they get prayed for. Most of time, everyone got filled with the initial sign of speaking in tongues. Sometimes, while the exhortation was going on, some would begin to manifest the gifts of the Spirit.

Remi Tejumola has been used by God severally to teach about the Holy Spirit and minister the baptism of the Spirit to many. According to one of his writings, he stepped into this dimension of ministry at Faith Clinic:

> As a new believer in Christ Jesus, I began to get into the Word to learn about the way of the Kingdom of God and His Christ; not for preaching, but for my own benefit. Doing that really helped in building a strong foundation for my Christian life.
>
> However, after I received the baptism in the Holy Spirit, I decided to learn how to minister the Holy Spirit baptism to others. I learnt how to do this through the books written on the subject by Revd Kenneth E. Hagin.
>
> I began to get involved in that area of ministry right there at the Faith Clinic, in Ibadan. It wasn't that I just received a special grace for it. That came later.
>
> One weekend, at the Faith Clinic, I was chosen to minister the Holy Spirit baptism to both the new converts and those who just got delivered from satanic oppression. I spent almost an hour to teach them what I've learnt, and suddenly, as if a cane was whipped through the crowd of people, like in a flash, they all got filled with the Holy Spirit and began to speak with tongues like they did in Acts 2:4.[15]

All glory to Jesus!

5

LABOURERS FOR
THE HARVEST

With testimonies of God's awesome power circulating the city every week, the people needing deliverance gradually began to increase. Very quickly, the situation resembled the one that Jesus encountered when He said, *"The harvest truly is plenteous, but the labourers are few."*[1] Certainly, Bro. Ibe must have followed the instruction of Jesus to *"Pray ye therefore the Lord of the harvest,"*[2] because one by one, labourers were sent to join in the great work of ministering to people.

A lot of this was due to the fact that God was moving in a sovereign way at Faith Clinic, and Bro. Ibe had a nature that enhanced what God was doing: he loved people, was approachable and very accessible. In the same way that he reached out to the lost and introduced them to Christ, he also had a heart for believers who were yearning to be used of God. He was able to attract a crop of young people to himself and provide leadership in the things of the Kingdom. He did not see himself as the centre of attraction; rather, he embraced the role of a mentor in the lives of those that God brought his way. With apostolic and fatherly insight into their potential, Bro. Ibe went all out to pour himself into them. Faith Clinic became a platform for their spiritual growth and ministry development.

Bear in mind that God was using Faith Clinic to restore the truth about the believers' authority over evil spirits. The kind of spiritual understanding and supernatural manifestations that occurred at Faith Clinic were not happening anywhere else – not with the same consistency and intensity, if at all. This alone was a mobilising factor for a lot of young people who were hungry for God.

The ministers came from different backgrounds and through different means; their experiences varied, but their motivation was the same – to love Jesus, serve God, win souls and destroy the works of the devil. As we look into Faith Clinic and Bro. Ibe through the perspectives and accounts of some of them, our understanding of how impacting the ministry was in those days, and how God used Bro. Ibe to shape the future landscape of Christian experience in Nigeria will be enriched (in the same way that the different gospel accounts by the disciples of Jesus Christ reveal and teach different aspects of Christ's person and ministry).

FUNKE ADETUBERU'S ACCOUNT

Funke Kolawole had become a believer in 1981 and was active in Faith Clinic from 1983 until the year she got married to Wale Adetuberu in 1987. Faith Clinic was all that she knew in those formative years of ministerial development. "Many of us," she recalls, "were youngsters who had become born-again for not too long."[3] Despite their spiritual adolescence, God used them alongside Bro. Ibe and they grew in their knowledge of God.

Funke testifies that Bro. Ibe was like a father to her and the other young ministers. He cared about their walk with God and encouraged them to keep growing in the faith. Since Faith Clinic was a para-church ministry, Bro. Ibe encouraged Funke and others to attend the Sunday evening service of *His Grace Evangelical Fellowship*. This worked perfectly, because the all-night meetings went on to the early hours of Sunday.

In the very early days, Funke sometimes joined Bro. Ibe to attend to people in his office. She witnessed many cases being referred to Faith Clinic from the doctor's office. "When the problems that people came to see him for defied medical explanation, we ended up praying for them," she recalls. "In the same way that doctors ask their patients leading questions in order to diagnose their medical history, we also asked questions to discern anything in their past or genealogy that contributed to their problem. We called it a *spiritumedical diagnosis!*"[4]

Funke shares the following testimonies:

> A couple came to see Dr. Ibe and I was also in the office. They came for a medical check-up. They were not having children. Dr. Ibe had asked many questions, but because she came from a Christian background, she seemed 'clean'. There was nothing suspicious we could pinpoint. She shared about the

engagement ceremony when she was getting married to her husband. On this day, which fell on the same day as the Osun festival, they were given a goat as a gift. This had been slaughtered on the day so it did not raise any alarms.

Somehow, my mind could not leave the issue about the goat. I perceived that it was significant. Noting my conviction, Dr. Ibe asked me to minister to her. Right there in the office, she began to manifest as a half-man, half-fish being. Water was oozing out of her body and the entire floor became drenched. We asked her to attend Faith Clinic and she was gloriously delivered. Now the couple are blessed with four children!

There was also a forty-year-old medical doctor at UCH who was yet unmarried. He came to Faith Clinic and I was asked to handle his case. Suddenly, in the course of ministering to him, he began to manifest as a woman, wriggling his waist and speaking in a high-pitch feminine voice. The Lord set him free and now he is happily married.[5]

Faith Clinic and the influence of Bro. Ibe are a vital part of the person Funke is in the Lord today.

MARCUS BENSON'S ACCOUNT

Marcus Benson was another young man who became close to Bro. Ibe. They met in 1985 and Bro. Ibe became the young Marcus' mentor. According to him, "Dr. Ibe saw in me what I did not see in myself. He discerned

God's call over my life and worked tirelessly on me."[6]

Marcus, who is now a Bishop in the Republic of Ireland, remembers vividly:

> "The ministry of Faith Clinic made you hunger for God. You could not hide in the crowd. By Saturday night, you had to 'deliver'. For this reason, you hungered for God and His power. There was an emphasis on righteousness, as well as fasting and prayer.
>
> Bro. Ibe was not scared of bringing people up to the centre stage. He gave all of us a chance to grow. He set a very high standard for us, because as a leader, he was highly anointed.
>
> In spite of this, Bro. Ibe came down to your level. You could never differentiate between Bro. Ibe and any of the other ministers. He was very accessible. After ministrations on Sunday morning, we all shared bread and coke. There was no difference whatsoever. Even during outside ministrations, we could enter his room freely. He was fond of cracking jokes.[7]

Bro. Ibeneme was committed to training the young ministers. He met with them every Friday for instruction and prayer. It was at this meeting that the rota for the various aspects of the all-night programme was decided. (The ministers would volunteer to take a portion of the programme—the first message, testimonies, offering, healing, second message or baptism of the Holy Spirit and Bro. Ibe would decide who took what session). The ministry format was unique for developing the gifting of the ministers. It was an atmosphere of love and discipline; and Marcus recalls that Bro. Ibe did not hesitate to suspend workers who messed up. "When you joined Faith Clinic in those days, you gave all," and it was not difficult to be sold out because the leader was a worthy example of selflessness.[8]

VICTOR AMOSUN'S ACCOUNT

Victor Amosun, who became one of Bro. Ibe's close associates, became aware of the ministry of Bro. Ibe in 1981. However, it was in 1985 that God "arranged" for him to encounter him and the ministry of Faith Clinic from a much closer range.

At that time, Victor was living with and being mentored by Rev. Yemi Ayodele, who was a close friend of Bro. Ibeneme. Every Saturday night, Rev. Ayodele went to Faith Clinic together with others like Rev. John Okposio, who used to travel from the College of Education, Ondo. Whenever they came back in the early hours of Sunday morning, they would share testimonies of deliverances that occurred in the meetings and ask him when he was going to visit.

One particular Saturday, Rev. Ayodele could not attend. He asked Victor to stand in for him and take the "first message" (the salvation message). "That was the beginning of my going to Faith Clinic," Victor recollects.

He remembers so much more of the person of Bro. Ibe and the ministry of Faith Clinic:

> Bro. Ibe, as we fondly called him, was an epitome of

love who lived practically what the Bible teaches. He was a man of integrity and virtue, who displayed servant-leadership for so many reasons.

At a time, I was having difficulty joining my family in the U.K. Bro. Ibe called me and said, 'I will have to go to England and see your wife because I cannot continue to look at you like this.' And he did. This was agape love in action.

Bro. Ibe was a result-oriented man. He never gave up on anybody or any situation. There was no false balance with him either of tribalism or ethnicity. He saw everybody through the eyes of Christ. He submitted himself to those he provided oversight for, to the extent that whenever he would go for an outside ministration, he would kneel in the middle of a circle with us while we prayed for him. When it came to interpersonal relationships, it was awesome relating with him. He was a selfless servant of God.

God used Faith Clinic to break the jinx surrounding spiritual warfare. It became clear that any Bible-believing Christian can exercise spiritual authority over the devil and take part in the mandate of the Great Commission as stated in Mark 16:15ff: *"...they shall cast out devils."*

We saw the Acts of the Apostles replay in the 20th century by those who dared to believe and act on what the Bible teaches. For instance, how do you explain a woman vomiting drawing pins that were used to block her fallopian tubes? After prayers for deliverance, she vomited two drawing pins and nine months later, she returned with a baby. How about a woman that felt an object was moving in her body and she had done series of medical investigations both in Nigeria and abroad without any solution. After she was prayed for, she vomited a lizard with all its parts complete. Another, classical one was a woman who had been carrying a pregnancy for years and eventually, she delivered a coconut. She was later dubbed "The coconut woman" wherever she testified of her miraculous deliverance. I cannot forget a woman who had hysterectomy surgery and later got pregnant and gave birth to a baby boy. I was at the dedication. All these miracles defied scientific explanation.[9]

Victor went on to pioneer a Bible class at Faith Clinic that developed into a Bible School and impacted the lives of hundreds of believers. (see the next chapter for full story). Today, he continues to minister the gospel of Christ on the mission field and is used of God to train believers in the ministry of deliverance.

REMI TEJUMOLA'S ACCOUNTS

There are a few ministers who openly acknowledge in their publications that their spiritual development is traceable to Faith Clinic. They assert that they were mentored by Bro. Ibe, were among the Faith Clinic ministers or they graduated from the Bible School.[10] However, no one, it seems, has written about and acknowledged his or her involvement with Faith Clinic as much as Remi Tejumola. His books and online blog have many accounts of his supernatural experiences at Faith Clinic (some of which we have already made reference to).

Remi joined Faith Clinic in 1985 and soon afterwards became closely acquainted with the ministry. He became one of the staff of Faith Clinic, the first resident minister, and he served till 1992. The story of how he was "recruited" into the workforce at Faith Clinic is interesting.

God pushed me into ministry work Himself. I didn't plan to be involved in it. He literally pushed me into it. I was minding my own business at the Faith Clinic holding inside the University College Hospital, Ibadan in 1985. It was a deliverance service, and that was about the third or fourth time I went for the programme. I returned there because it was as if I was seeing the Bible live - very interesting! I saw people saved, healed, delivered from evil spirits (demons), and baptised in the Holy Spirit, in Jesus' name! That name works!

During that service, one of the workers came out, and announced, 'If you have come to join us to help minister to people, raise up your hand.' (I didn't really hear what he said). My right hand just went up as if someone pushed it up! The brother said further, 'Stand up!' I stood up, and thought, 'What did he say?' (Then what he said dawned on me). I then thought that I will explain to him that I haven't really come to do that, thinking that, 'Maybe these other people have been invited specially for this.' But there was no room for explanation as we were ushered out of that auditorium to a place where we were prayed for in preparation to minister to people with various needs. That was really how it began with me in the ministry.[11]

After that "accidental" beginning, Remi continued to minister at Faith Clinic and has remained a firebrand for God even after he left the ministry. He wrote about how God began to use him to minister healing to others.

A few weeks later, during the ministry's preparatory prayer session prior to ministering to the people, an elderly woman among us, who was suffering from a terrible migraine headache, stepped out into the middle and requested for prayer. The brother (Greg Alabi) leading us in the prayer session instructed us to jointly pray in tongues for her. When he rounded us off, he asked me to pray for her. I pointed my forefinger towards her head and commanded, 'In the name of Jesus, headache, be gone from her!' To my amazement, an unseen power picked her off the ground, and threw her away from me! She landed on the floor with a thud, got off the ground and shouted that the headache was gone! I looked at my fore-finger and thought, 'What?!'[12]

In his book, *The Holy Ghost Invasion*, Remi shares some insight on what it meant to be part of the Faith Clinic ministry team on a Saturday night.

Many times when I was a worker with the Faith Clinic Nigeria (led by Reverend (Dr.) I.K.U. Ibeneme of blessed memory), we would minister all night long, casting out devils. In those days, we would feel tired in the night having worked all day. When we were about to start ministering to the people, we would ask God to strengthen us, and suddenly, we would actually feel strength flow into our beings. As a result, we would be able to minister tirelessly throughout the night till the early hours of the next day. The Holy Ghost will strengthen you when the need arises and you ask Him.[13]

Not all of the Faith Clinic ministers were young people, as one of Remi's blog posts, dedicated to the memory of one of the older ministers, reveal:

A senior friend just went home to be with the Lord, Pastor Patrick Ezekude Obaze. He was aged 78 years old.

I got to know him in 1985 after I became a part of the Faith Clinic which was founded by Rev. (Dr.) I.K.U. Ibeneme of blessed memory.

Uncle 'Bobo' Obaze, as was fondly called by Dr. Ibeneme, was one of the numerous workers that the Faith Clinic had in those days in the mid-80s. All the workers came from different churches and ministries, and were of various ages and giftings.

In spite of his age, he was simple and humble. He was easy to get along with, and very kind. He loved Jesus and was as excited about Him as anyone of us was who were much younger than he was.

Like other workers of the ministry he was involved in deliverance ministrations. He often travelled with Dr. Ibeneme for outside ministrations. He also had a special love to minister the Holy

Ghost baptism. He had great success in this area of ministry. I know it because I was also used of God in this area in the same ministry.

Between the last time that I saw him ministering at the Faith Clinic and now, I found out that God has used him to minister life to many people, as was testified of at his wake-keep yesterday. He was laid to rest today at his hometown.

Adieu, Uncle "Bobo" Obaze![14]

AUNTY PHEOBE'S ACCOUNT

Aunty Pheobe, well-known at Faith Clinic in those days, especially in the Bible School, lived in Kano prior to her association with Bro. Ibe. She was led to Christ and discipled by Professor Bill Isaacs-Sodeye, Bro. Ibe's former lecturer at University of Ibadan. The Professor also stood firmly with her when she lost her husband in Kano — the incident that led to her salvation.

When she was to relocate to Ibadan, her father-in-the-Lord recommended that she goes to see his own "Papa," Dr. Ibeneme. Being a big city, she wondered how or where she would locate this "Dr. Ibeneme."

On settling down in Ibadan, she was invited to attend an outreach that was being held at the Premier Hotel; and this is where her Faith Clinic story begins to unfold:

I parked my car at Premier's parking lot, and as I was walking up the hill to the hotel, there was this tall man, standing at the entrance of the hotel. As I looked at him from afar, the Spirit of the Lord told me, 'That is Ibeneme.' As I moved closer, he too was also walking down the stairs.

"You must be Sis. Yetunde from Kano," he said. "And you must be Dr. Ibeneme," I replied. That was it! The beginning of a very beautiful relationship!

Bro. Ibe then told me about Faith Clinic. "Just come and look," he said.

"Ok, I will come and look," I replied. And I went, and I looked, and I couldn't stop looking from that day! I was too fascinated. "This God," I wondered back then, "is He this powerful?" I watched so many deliverances. In some of them, the devils will be speaking through people. It was just so fascinating! While some people would come to Faith Clinic and be sleeping, I could not sleep!

Eventually, I decided to go through deliverance, and afterwards, I came alive in the spirit. It was like the spiritual things already in me came to life. In Kano, Professor Isaacs-Sodeye had trained us in the word and in the Christian way. However, after the deliverance, the word of God in me welled up to the extent that I ended up in the teaching arm of Faith Clinic.[15]

MY MOTHER'S ACCOUNT

My parents, Kunle and Esther Odulaja, were dedicated ministers at Faith Clinic. The account of my mother, Esther Olulaja,[16] is enlightening:

Faith Clinic was where I made my public confession

of faith. Rev. Moses Aransiola was the one taking the salvation message on this faithful day in August 1986. Since that day, I frequented Faith Clinic with my late husband. It was at UCH at the time.

I was also ministered to and experienced deliverance at the meetings. I had taken one of my nieces for ministration and ended up needing deliverance myself.

During one of the visits, I heard a voice speak to me and say, "Man shall not live by bread alone but by every word that proceeds from the mouth of God." Prompted by this word, I enrolled at the Bible School and attended faithfully for 18 months. There were two classes that spanned this time. After I finished at the Bible School, I joined the ministers. I sometimes interpreted or took one of the sessions. I also led songs, especially during the deliverance session. During the deliverance session, after an exhortation to prepare the hearts and minds of the people, we go into what we call 'raking', which was open addressing of demonic entities and breaking of strongholds. Usually, many people start manifesting at this point and get taken out for ministration.

I remember the testimony of the "coconut woman." I was officiating on the day she gave her testimony. She was formerly a prophetess in the Celestial Church of Christ, but was also a highly-ranked agent in the kingdom of darkness. Due to her diligence and dedication to the secret world she belonged to, she was given the title "elemele meje."

She probably came to do some harm when the Holy Spirit arrested her and she was ministered to. When she testified, she brought some items to be burnt – a calabash used to collect blood, a white clothe, a padlock etc. That day, all the items she brought were burnt to ashes.

We usually met on Friday for prayer. At this meeting, ministers were allocated for different sessions of the Saturday programme. Those who will participate from the pulpit usually go on a three-day fast. I learnt to fast at Faith Clinic.

Bro. Ibe was a workaholic. He also loved all his ministers. He was able to carry everyone along. He was also very jovial. After deliverance sessions, we all got together and ate bread! He was just like the way Christ was with His disciples. If you had not met him before, you may not be able to point him out from among the ministers. He gave all his ministers a free hand.[17]

KUNLE OLANIRAN'S ACCOUNT

Kunle Olaniran is one of the longest-serving members of staff at Faith Clinic, even till this day. The story of how he joined the team is heart-warming.

I came to Faith Clinic in 1985 through the recommendation of a friend. My first son, who was six at the time, had been suffering from asthma since the age of nine months. I was known in UCH because of our frequent visits for treatment. In 1982, I was posted to work in UCH's medical library from UI, and had known Dr. Ibeneme facially as one of the doctors who visited the library for reference books.

One of the medical students, who was aware of my son's problem and how it weighed terribly on me, recommended that I attend Faith Clinic. He said I needed to attend to the problem spiritually and not just medically. He testified about the glorious things that were happening there. I had become a Christian in 1975 and had read the Bible many times; but I had never heard or seen the things that the student was sharing with me. Out of curiosity, I decided to attend; besides, the hall that Faith Clinic was using was not far from my office.

I came to the all-night meeting with a letter to show Dr. Ibeneme the problems my son was facing. I also came with my son. On getting there, I was disappointed to find that the doctor was not there. He had gone for an outside ministration in Port Harcourt. To make matters worse, the person leading the meeting made a hurtful comment. He said, "If you have come to see Dr. Ibeneme, I am sorry you will be disappointed. But the God that Dr. Ibeneme serves is here; His name is Jesus! He will deliver you tonight and you will go home with joy." I was not comforted and just wanted to see what would happen.

When it was time for ministrations, I sent my son forward to be prayed for. When it got to his turn, the minister who was to attend to him said, "Where is the mother or father of this child? Who brought this child?" I had to stand and identify myself. Without any time to narrate his problems, the minister said, "Your boy is not the one with the problem; you are the one that needs to be prayed for." Before I could comprehend what he had said, they began to pray for me. I did not know that I had problems with demonic oppression! I went plump on the floor and the ministers conducted deliverance for me.

After I was gloriously delivered, they beckoned to my son and prayed a simple prayer of healing for him. "Is that it?" I wondered. But to the glory of God, that was the last time he had any asthmatic attack! I could not believe how simple the process was!

After that encounter, I began to read the Bible in a new way. I saw the way Jesus prayed for the sick and cast out devils, and realised that He was still doing the same today. I had just experienced His love and power in a tangible way and was so grateful. I went back the following week and registered to attend the Bible School.

One day, there was a problem with the lightening and the ministers were struggling to sort out the problem. Meanwhile, the people who had gathered were being led to pray against the demonic powers that wanted to hinder the meeting. Being an electrician, I moved closer to the ministers and asked what the problem was.

"Go into the meeting and pray!" I was told, but I stayed there to observe what they were doing. Each time they put in a bulb or make a connection, the fuse will blow.

I summoned the courage again, moved close to the ministers and told them I was an electrician. "You are?" they said. "Come and have a look then."

I had a tester in my pocket and before long, discovered where the problem was. The moment I fixed it, the lights came back on and there were shouts of joy in the hall. "Praise God! The devil is a liar! We have overcome the demonic powers of darkness!"

"It wasn't the devil," I thought to myself; "It was only a wrong electrical connection!"

Dr. Ibeneme was in the meeting that night, and he asked for the person who fixed the light. When I came over to him, he recognised me. "You are an electrician?" he asked. "From today on, you will be responsible for all our lightening!" He said it with authority.

That is how I joined the Technical Department of Faith Clinic and I am still there till today. When we moved to the Stadium, I will be there from 11am, setting up for the evening event.[18]

MIKE AYODELE'S ACCOUNT

Mike Ayodele joined Faith Clinic in 1987. He was a Muslim — his father practised Islam but his mother was a Christian. Before coming to Faith Clinic, he had followed his mother to church because he wanted to sit for some exams and was praying to God for success. However, he saw God in action at Faith Clinic, got convicted of sin and consequently gave his life to Christ. Not only is he still in the Lord, he remains a minister at Faith Clinic till this day.

Mike had a personal encounter with Bro. Ibe that left a lasting impression upon his heart.

> Bro. Ibe was an epitome of love and humility. There is no way you would not want to draw close to someone like him. When my mother died in 1992, Bro. Ibe came to visit me where I lived in the interior of Ibadan. He met me lying down on the pavement, and asked the people around not to wake me up. I was really overcome by grief at the demise of my mother. Bro. Ibe just sat there quietly beside me. It was in my dreams that I felt the presence of some-one with me.
>
> When I woke up, I was shocked to find Bro. Ibe by my side. He simply said, "Mike, how are you? And how are the arrangements?" We had not done any arrangements whatsoever by this time because of the sorrow. Bro. Ibe gathered my family together, ministered to us and comforted us. From that day, I renewed my commitment to Christ. I concluded that Jesus was worth following because of the example of Bro. Ibe.[19]

This testimony shows that Bro. Ibe was one of the few that could say, like Paul, "Be ye followers of me, even as I also am of Christ."[20]

Mike also testifies of the power of God at Faith Clinic.

We saw too many miracles to recount. Cancers got healed. Mad people got delivered. There was a person who had a wound for many years. Doctors had done many surgeries but had found nothing responsible for the wound. After deliverance at Faith Clinic, he went home and had a dream. In his dream, someone came to him, touched his wound and removed something from it. When he woke up, he saw something like a bone in the wound and effortlessly removed it by himself. Two weeks later, the wound healed by itself. Glory to God![21]

MARY BELLO'S ACCOUNT

Mary Bello[22] was another former Muslim who got saved in 1977. Living at the time in the North of Nigeria, she endured much persecution from her family because of her conversion to Christianity. However, her conviction about her faith and relationship with God was so strong that she could not stop testifying about Christ. This, of course, did not help matters for her. She was moved from one secondary school to another because of her relentless sharing of the good news. Even when it was dangerous to reach out to others, she found a way to witness.

For instance, she created an album, not of personal pictures, but of the message of salvation. So when people came to greet her, she will hand them the album, which explained graphically the message of salvation. With her guests engaged with the pictures and the Scripture quotations, she will explain what it meant to be a sinner and to be saved. Many got saved through this strategy.

Apart from preaching about Christ, she also prayed for those who needed healing. Many came to her to be prayed for. At times, she got called to see those who needed prayer. It was during one of such "missions" that she saw a demonic manifestation for the first time. She did not know what it was, but the lady she was called to pray for was really manifesting. "I knew I had authority to take charge of the situation, so I prayed and commanded that she got well."[23] Suddenly, she became her normal self and many who witnessed the instant change gave their lives to Christ. It was much later, after joining Faith Clinic, that Mary understood that it was a demonic manifestation that she dealt with on this day.

Mary was persuaded by friends to leave the North and pursue her tertiary education in the South of Nigeria. Admitted into the College of Education in Ibadan, she continued to preach the gospel and lead people to Christ. She also became a leader in the college fellowship. It was at the fellowship that she first witnessed the ministry of Bro. Ibe, when he was invited to speak as a guest.

> I cannot recall what he preached on, but as he minis-
> tered and started praying for people, demons were
> manifesting everywhere. People were screaming;
> some were rolling on the floor. I had never seen any-
> thing like it before! "What kind of anointing is
> this?" I had asked myself.[24]

Fascinated and challenged by what they witnessed that day, a few brethren from the fellowship, including Mary, decided to visit Faith Clinic. From this first visit, they became frequent attendees at Faith Clinic. Mary attended virtually every Saturday. When she graduated in 1985, she joined Faith Clinic fully as one of the ministers. Her testimony shows how impacting the ministry of Faith Clinic was in her life and the lives of many.

At first, it was just a few who attended Faith Clinic, but before long, the whole auditorium was full. All this happened without any advertisement or publicity.

There was a core of us who were close to Bro. Ibe, all of us young people who were passionate about God. We prayed with him, travelled with him and ministered with him. I learnt a lot from him and from Faith Clinic.

The explosion at Faith Clinic is akin to the experience of the woman of Samaria. After she encountered the Lord, she ran into the city with the testimony: "Come and see a man who told me everything I ever did!" Her testimony drew the entire community to Christ. In the same way, those who received the touch of God in Faith Clinic went everywhere testifying about the power of God and bringing others who needed the intervention of God in their lives.

Faith Clinic started from Bro. Ibe's house, but soon, it was no longer big enough to contain the people coming. From his house we moved to UCH and from UCH to Adamasingba stadium. At the stadium, people flooded from everywhere. There were too many cases to catalogue or document.

I concluded that demons are real; also, that those who get delivered should be taught the ways and principles of God. The need to teach people the Word of God birthed the Bible School.

I knew Bro. Ibe very well. I got close to him and his family. Viewing him from close range, I know that he did not have any skeleton in his cupboard. He was an open man and an epitome of love.

He taught us to fast and pray. It was not uncommon for us to fast for three days before going for a ministration. Bro. Ibe was truly anointed. I discovered that demons cannot stand an atmosphere that is charged with the anointing. They also get uncomfortable when those who can discern them are around. So many times, Bro. Ibe will be ministering and demons will be screaming out of people.

I remember a time I was leading worship. I remember the simple song I raised:

O Lord my God

How excellent is your name

In all the earth

How excellent is your name

As I sang this song, many demons began to manifest with people screaming and falling everywhere.

At Faith Clinic it was not all about Bro. Ibe. God used us to minister to people and the number of ministers steadily increased.

One day at UCH, we were ministering to people one by one. Usually, some of the ministers will be in front of the auditorium and we will randomly call those seated to come forward for prayer. When they start to manifest, they are taken to another place where other ministers will continue the deliverance ministration. I was quite smallish in those days, but demons do not fear our physical stature as they do our spiritual stature. I remember calling a lady forward and I simply held her hands and commanded any demonic influence in her life to be broken in the name of Jesus. Suddenly, she loosed her hands from mine, screamed and fell on the floor. She manifested fiercely for a few minutes and then came to herself. She looked at herself on the floor and then looked up at me.

Later, she testified that as she sat among those waiting for prayer, she was saying to herself, "What can this little girl do? I would prefer Bro. Ibeneme to pray for me." She confessed that she felt disappointed when I was the one who beckoned to her, but was astonished to see herself on the floor after my simple prayer. She concluded that it was not about Bro. Ibe but about God. She went and brought more people to Faith Clinic.

It was also the same when we ministered the baptism of the Holy Spirit to people. People gradually understood that it was not the person who laid hands on you, but God who longed to fill them with His Spirit.

There were even times when Bro. Ibe, tired and exhausted, dozed off while laying hands on people and praying in the spirit. Even in this state, the person being prayed for will be manifesting and demons will be fleeing out of them.

Bro. Ibe had a very large heart. He exhibited practical love. He always went the extra mile to care for us. After meetings or ministrations, he will usually take us in his car and drop everyone in their homes. This gave our parents the confidence to release us for the work; they were assured of our safety. When I left school, he was so concerned that I got an employment. He took me to a few places in search of work.[25]

CHRISTOPHER OKARTER'S ACCOUNT

The story of Christopher Okarter is one of the most dramatic accounts of how God rallied an army of ministers around Bro. Ibe and used them so mightily in Faith Clinic.

Bro. Okarter joined Faith Clinic in 1985. He had gotten saved in 1978 and was a member of the Assemblies of God Mission. Months before joining Faith Clinic, he had a startling dream that he did not understand at the time. In the dream, he saw a big Cathedral full of people. Just outside the Cathedral, he was among eight people standing in a line, side-by-side, all dressed in white. One after the other, each person got told: "This is your leader." The appointed leader would then come and stand beside the protégé, awaiting their turn to be called into the Cathedral. When Bro. Okarter was shown his leader, the person that came to stand by him was a tall, fair-complexioned black man with a short beard.

As each person got summoned, his assigned leader would lead him into the Cathedral to deliver his message. Bro. Okarter was the eighth person on the queue. However, just before his turn, his tall leader said to him, "I am going ahead of you and will be waiting for you at the altar. When it is your turn, just start coming into the Cathedral."

Wondering how he could face the crowd inside, Bro. Okarter objected. "I can't come by myself." The leader insisted and then went inside the Cathedral. Bro. Okarter stood there petrified. When it was his turn to go in, he stayed outside. Everyone was waiting for his arrival. The leader came back out and was furious that he was still hesitating. "What are you still doing here? Everybody is waiting for you. Start coming now!" he commanded.

Reluctantly, Bro. Okarter followed him inside. He saw the others who were once standing with him outside with trays of rewards for their obedience and ministry (the trays were covered with a white clothe and he could not see what each person had received). At this, he woke up, not understanding what the dream meant.

A few weeks later, the women's ministry of his local assembly were having a week-long programme. One of the sessions was devoted to Family Planning, and the guest speaker was Dr. Ibeneme. Bro. Okarter attended this event but arrived quite late. As he entered the hall and sat at the back, the guest speaker whom he had never seen before spotted him and said, "Young man, make sure you see me at the end of the meeting." Bro. Okarter did not immediately recognise that the guest doctor fitted the description of his "leader" in the dream.

After the meeting, Bro. Ibe came straight to him and extended an invitation to him. "I want you to come to Faith Clinic, at UCH. Come and see the things that God is doing there."

Bro. Okarter assured the doctor that he would come. However, after he left the meeting, he wondered why he should. He was already grounded in the AOG doctrines and was not accustomed to going about in search of sensational manifestations. For these reasons, he did not honour the doctor's invitation.

A few times after this encounter, Bro. Okarter will bump into Bro. Ibe and each time, Bro. Ibe would recognise him and say, "When are you coming to Faith Clinic? I am expecting you." Each time, Bro. Okarter would promise to come but immediately dismiss it from his heart.

The fateful day came, a Saturday, when Bro. Okarter once again met the doctor at Mokola market. This time, Bro. Ibe said with authority, "You must come to Faith Clinic today!" Unlike other times, Bro. Okarter could not ignore the invitation. Throughout the day, he kept hearing in his heart: "You must go to Faith Clinic today." And he did.

When he arrived at the lecture hall at UCH, the whole place was filled, so he sat at the second-to-the-last row of seats. He wondered what was special about the meeting and was ready to scrutinise everything that was done. He noticed that things were done in sequence. There was first a time of worship, then a message of salvation, some testimonies and then a healing message.

When it got to the healing message, the person handling the session, after sharing the word, began to minister in the word of knowledge. The minister will call out a condition, identify the person concerned, and pray a simple prayer; shortly afterwards, the afflicted person will claim to have been healed. Not accustomed to that kind of operation, Bro. Okarter considered it all a game.

The minister called out someone who was deaf in one ear, placed his hand in the person's bad ear and commanded the ear to open. The man began to rejoice and said he could now hear clearly. At this point, Bro. Okarter needed to be sure this was genuine. He began to pray to God: "If all this is true, prove it to me." Incidentally, he was having sharp pains in his sides because of an ulcer condition. "Make the minister call my condition, for only then would I believe in all this."

Before he could finish his inward conversation, the minister called out: "There is someone here with burning sensations in his sides due to ulcer. Come out and the Lord will heal you."

Shocked at the instant response to his fleece, he got up from his seat. Another man had also gotten up and they were both approaching the front. However, the minister pointed to the other man and said: "It's not you sir. Go back to your seat." Needless to say, Bro. Okarter was instantly healed.

As the custom was at Faith Clinic, those who get born again and those came for the first time were usually invited for deliverance prayers. When Bro. Okarter got prayed for, he was shocked to find himself manifesting violently. That night, he was delivered of a spirit of rage and violence that was a trait of his family background.

It was during the deliverance ministration that Bro. Ibe saw him. The moment Bro. Ibe spotted Bro. Okarter, he joined in the deliverance and saw to it that he was completely free. Thereafter, something unusual happened. Bro. Ibe told him to start ministering to someone who needed prayer. Bro. Okarter protested that he did not know how.

"I'm here with you. Just start praying in the name of Jesus," the doctor said. "Watch me and do what I do. If you make a mistake, I will correct you." And that was it. Bro. Okarter was used of God, under the supervision of Bro. Ibe, to successfully cast out demons from people all through the night!

Whilst all this was happening, he recalled a dream he had in 1978, the dream that got him searching for Christ and led to his conversion. In that dream, an angel had brought him into a field, like a wilderness, where he had seen so many people bound with chains, looking helpless and destitute like prisoners. After a while, he was taken up by the angel into the clouds. When they got to a particular level, he saw two mighty hands coming out of the clouds. The hands were shining like the brightness of the sun, but he did not see the image of the person whose hands were outstretched. The angel that carried him brought him towards the hands and the Person in the clouds embraced him, with the angel standing by. He was then taken back to the earth and he woke up.

So, on his first visit to Faith Clinic, both of Bro. Okarter's dreams began to make sense – the dream he had in 1978 about the field full of captives and the more recent one about the leader who urged him into the Cathedral. The course of his life and the leader who would walk with him on this divine path became clear in one day.

From that day onwards, Bro. Ibe began to pour himself into Bro. Okarter. They spent a lot of time sharing together and Bro. Ibe exposed him to the things of God. He made sure that Bro. Okarter always accompanied him to ministrations around the country.[26]

* * *

It is not possible to recount the experiences of all the people that God used in Faith Clinic. The stories are as diverse as the people themselves. Whether it was "the Twelve" who were closer to Bro. Ibe (not the exact number) or "the Seventy" who also partook of the grace of the ministry, they all have their peculiar stories; they found in Faith Clinic the opportunity to grow in their walk with God. As Remi Tejumola wrote, "At (Faith Clinic) every weekend, we experienced the raw power of God in salvation, healings, deliverances and the Holy Ghost baptism. Imagine being raised under such an atmosphere in ministry work!"[27]

6

WORD EXPLOSION
AT THE STADIUM!

M onth in, month out, the attendance at Faith Clinic continued to grow. Just as Bro. Ibe's residence could not contain the people and they had to move to UCH, the PSM lecture hall soon became too small for the number of people that were coming every weekend. As the crowds grew, so also did the ministry activities.

The main ministry operation and programme was quite effective in bringing people into the faith, for delivering them from bondage and baptising them in the Holy Spirit. However, while still at UCH, the need for another dimension of ministry soon became obvious.

Those who received deliverance subsequently and consistently brought others to be ministered to. While their invitees underwent deliverance, and with nothing else to do from around 1am in the middle of the night, some went to sleep in their cars; many became spectators, while others simply loitered around. Truly, the deliverance sessions were an exciting sight! There was so much to see. Sometimes, the demons tried to put up a "fight" or resist being sent out of their victims; at other times, they were too talkative and wanted to converse before leaving. Even Bro. Ibe once admitted that in the early days, they sometimes got carried away by the sensational manifestations.[1] With time and maturity, these unnecessary distractions were curtailed. The focus of the ministry remained on Jesus Christ and on completing the task of ministering deliverance to the captives.

So, in order to discourage loitering and idle chatting, the introduction of a Bible class for those who had been delivered was suggested. The leadership deliberated on this idea and it was readily adopted. Not only would it address the problem of reducing onlookers during deliverance ministrations, it was a perfect solution to a pressing need. It had become crucial for the saints to be instructed in the precepts of the faith. How would they maintain their deliverance if they are not equipped in the Word? Bro. Ibe was interested in people growing in their walk with God, and not endlessly attending Faith Clinic for spiritual check-up and deliverance sessions.

This is how the teaching arm of Faith Clinic was launched in 1985 at the UCH venue. Victor Amosun was given the responsibility of leading this new arm of the ministry. At this early stage, it was just like a Bible class. It afforded people the opportunity to learn the Word of God instead of stand around idly while the deliverance sessions were going on.

Aunty Pheobe later joined the new teaching arm of the

ministry. At a point, Victor Amosun and Aunty Pheobe were the two teachers taking the classes. She remembers those early days vividly:

> We did not call it a school at that time. We just called it Teaching. I started working with Bro. Victor Amosun. It was only the two of us then. He would say, "Sis. Pheobe, you will teach so-and-so topic next week," and I would go home to prepare. Somehow we would meet during the week and review what I'd written and the Bible references. He would say, "Why don't you add this; why don't you add that." So, I also grew just being part of the Teaching class.
>
> Before we knew it, those who wanted to attend the teaching were much more than what the two of us could handle. Other people began to join us and the operation soon metamorphosed into a school. What started as one class became multiple classes functioning simultaneously.[2]

Victor Amosun and Greg Alabi were part of the team who put the original curriculum of the school together. They were also among the foundational teaching staff.[3] Just like the main meetings, the school experienced dynamic growth. It began with two classes – the X Class and Y Class. These two classes lasted nine months each.

Some of the first set of graduates were recruited as teachers for subsequent classes. In the same way that the Lord was adding to the numbers of those who ministered deliverance, he also strengthened the teaching staff with able, committed and dedicated teachers.

By the time Faith Clinic moved to the stadium, the students were so many, that they had to split the school into five classes that spanned three months each. The classes were dubbed the F-A-I-T and H classes (after the acronym *faith*).

With an explosion in the number of students, visiting lecturers were also engaged, including Dr. Dele Amosun, Pastor Abiodun Ilori, Pastor David Ayo Salawu, Sister Lara Adedeji, Sister Anu Adejuwon among others.[4]

The Faith Clinic Bible School was given the same level of attention as the main arm of the ministry – if not more. A high level of devotion was expected from the students. Before moving from one class to the other, they wrote an assessment and had to be deemed fit to continue. Aunty Pheobe, who had much grace in administration, was an asset to the school. She kept the records of all the students, who was in what class; who had completed what assessment, etc. The operation was orderly, meticulous and effective.

> The impact of the teachings was so much because they were hands-on courses that were being taught, which you can practice on a day-to-day basis. Initially, no fee was charged, but at a point in time we had to charge a token fee of N20 (Twenty Naira) for commitment from the students. The School graduated many students that returned to their churches and began to make impact, which was the original intention. Also, it became a prerequisite for anybody that wanted to join the work force of the ministry to pass through the School.[5]

Segun Akintola first attended Faith Clinic in 1987. After witnessing the manifestation of God's glory and undergoing deliverance, he was left with a zeal and hunger to know more about God. He immediately enrolled for the Bible School. The X Class, as he remembers it, dealt with Basic principles of Christianity; while the Y Class focused on The Rudiments and Ethics of Ministry. Segun finished the course in two years and afterwards, joined the team of ministers.[6]

Temitope Mene[7] joined the school in 1991 and went through the F-A-I-T-H classes. Her tattered notes of more than twenty years reveal a lot about the teaching regime at Faith Clinic. The handwritten notes were not only detailed, there is evidence that the lecturers inspected them at the beginning of each lesson. Students were mandated to take notes and the lecturers appended their signatures to each lesson after inspecting them.

Mike Ayodele joined the Bible School after committing his life to Christ at Faith Clinic. He was part of the second set of students that graduated from the school. He shared that after the Y Class, the students were taken for practical deliverance sessions. This entailed them ministering deliverance under the supervision of their teachers during the main deliverance sessions. Bro. Ibe would usually share a Hausa proverb with the students before their "practical" deliverance session. He would say: *Ga firi, ga doke, me hao,* which meant: *This is the horse; this is the field; now let's see how well you can ride!* Of course, there were always enough people needing ministry during the deliverance sessions.

Meanwhile, members of Mike's family, mainly Muslims, had been deriding his newly found faith. They discarded the manifestations at Faith Clinic and claimed that Bro. Ibe had a magic ring that he used to perform miracles and cast out devils. Mike was, therefore, eager to see what would happen during the practical session, since he had only been taught the Word of God and was given no ring for casting out devils.

> I was given someone to pray for. As I stood before the person, I quoted the Scripture that said, "Out of your belly shall flow the rivers of living water" and laid my hands on the person. Instantly, she began to manifest and soon after, began to vomit blood. I was so shocked I nearly ran away! From that time, I knew that the power of God was real.[8]

In spite of the high standards at the Faith Clinic Bible School, hundreds of students graduated successfully. Unfortunately, some dropped off mid-way and did not complete the course.[9]

Some who completed the curriculum joined the Faith Clinic ministers. Most went back to their churches and used the knowledge they had received to serve the Lord – which was one of the objectives and visions of the school. Eternity will reveal the impact that the teaching arm of Faith Clinic had on a generation of believers in Nigeria.

A browse through Temitope's over-twenty-year-old notes, which covered the first three classes (F-A-I), showed the breadth of the teaching at the school. Below are some of the topics they covered:

F-CLASS

Sanctification

Process of sanctification

Effects of God's word for sanctification

Man

Spirit, soul & body

Faith

Conflict between the senses

Process of developing faith

Repentance

Steps of repentance

Baptisms

Types of baptisms

Significance of baptisms

Holy Ghost baptism

Laying on of hands

Significance of laying on of hands

Resurrection of the dead

Death

Resurrection

Eternal judgement

7 Types of judgement

Consecration

The Holy Spirit

Effects of the Holy Spirit on the believer

Dependence on the Holy Spirit

Holy Spirit in the life of the Church

Emblems of the Holy Spirit

Prayer

How to pray

A-CLASS

New birth and justification

    Why we need to be reborn

    Justification

Concluding the past

    Four areas to conclude

    Why we should put off the old man

    How do we go about it?

    Works of the flesh

Newness of life and walking in His steps

    Attaining newness of life

    Walking in His steps

    What mind should be in us?

Studying the Bible

    Purpose of the Bible

    How to learn Bible truth

    Methods of studying the Bible

Prayer

    What is prayer?

    Why do we pray?

    Where can we pray?

    When should we pray?

    How do we pray?

    Hindrances to prayer

    Does God answer prayer?

    Examples of prayer

    Prayer promises

Thanksgiving, praise and worship

Witnessing

    Definition of witnessing

    Who has to witness?

To whom do you witness?

How to open the talk

Dos in witnessing

Preparing for a witnessing visit

Your approach in witnessing

Useful Bible verses for witnessing

Hindrances in witnessing

Quiet Time

Definition of Quiet Time

The place of Quiet Time

Materials for Quiet Time

Why Quiet Time is necessary

Procedures in Quiet Time

Importance and benefits of Quiet Time

Consecration

Items to be consecrated (spirit, soul and body)

Godhead (Trinity)

Functions of the Godhead

God the Father, God the Son, God the Holy Spirit

Fellowship

Who to fellowship with

How to fellowship

Benefits of fellowship

How we can fellowship with one another

Why we need to fellowship

Sanctification

I-CLASS

Fruit of the Spirit

    Instrument of growing the fruit

    Conditions for fruit-bearing

    How to abide in the Lord Jesus

Fasting

    Definition of fasting

    Is fasting biblical?

    Types of fasting

    Duration of fasting

    Why do we fast?

    Who should fast?

Giving

    Types of giving

    Teaching on Malachi 3:8-14

    Offering

    Miscellaneous giving

    Vows and pledges

    Seven examples of common vows

    Seed of faith

    Principles of giving

    Scriptural rules of giving

Spiritual growth

    Babyhood

    Childhood

    Manhood

Spiritual gifts

    Revelational gifts

    Power gifts

    Inspirational gifts

Discipleship

    Cost of discipleship

    Marks of discipleship

    How a disciple can grow

Faith Dynamics

    Basic ingredients of faith

    How faith works

    Different levels of faith

    The spiritual gift of faith

    How faith grows

    Hindrances to faith

    Blessings of having faith

Divine healing

    God's plan for healing

    Methods of healing

    Hindrances to healing

Divine guidance (knowing the will of God)

    Guidance through the Scriptures

    Guidance through the Holy Spirit

The power of the tongue

    Creative power of the tongue

    Confession

Spiritual Warfare

    Weapons of our warfare

* * *

As Bro. Ibe and the Faith Clinic team travelled for "outside ministrations" (see chapter 8), there was a steady increase in the demand for instruction and training in the ministry of deliverance. Responding to this demand, the Faith Clinic Bible School was opened in Lagos and Enugu simultaneously. The Lagos branches was anchored by Dr. Evbuoma, while the Enugu work started through the efforts of Dr. (Mrs.) Edith Nwosu and her husband, Mr. Emenike Nwosu. Countless numbers of students are now established in the ministry due to the impact of the Faith Clinic Bible School.[10]

7

CRITICISM, SCEPTICISM AND OPPOSITION

Historically, the moves of God in revival, especially those that come with some sort of unusual, physical manifestations (and they almost all do!), are usually looked upon with doubt and contempt by spectators. The religious community are normally in the forefront of this hostility. The disciples on the day of Pentecost were thought to be drunk;[1] the manifestations at Azusa were called a "Weird Babel of Tongues."[2] Even Christ was constantly derided; He was thought to be casting devils out "by Beelzebub, the prince of the devils."[3] Faith Clinic and Bro. Ibe had their fair share of critics and sceptics.

CRITICS

On the surface, some of the reasons why some ministers struggled to endorse the Faith Clinic movement seemed valid: "How can a Christian be possessed by an evil spirit?" "The death of Jesus Christ on the cross is the ultimate and conclusive deliverance from the kingdom of darkness." These were theological issues, ones that needed theological answers. Bro. Ibe, indeed, taught extensively on the subject of deliverance and also substantiated the teachings with the many signs that accompanied them.[4]

Constructive criticism can actually help to test the validity of a claim and lead the open-hearted to further clarity. However, many critics blindly reject any kind of explanation. Sadly, those who took this position frequently spoke openly and cynically against Bro. Ibe. Some preached against the move from the pulpit. Others warned their members not go anywhere near Faith Clinic. In fact, some of the Faith Clinic ministers were ostracised by their churches.[5]

For instance, the drama group of the AOG church where Jonah Mbadugha and Christopher Okarter were members once narrated the experiences they were having. After some of their dramas, especially the ones that depicted the devil and evil spirits, they usually had spiritual attacks. Knowing that Bro. Jonah and Bro. Okarter attended Faith Clinic, they asked for help and were eager to be ministered to.

Brother Jonah recalls that they spent three days teaching them about some spiritual truth about the spirit realm and the authority that believers have in Christ. Afterwards, they fixed a day for the deliverance ministration. It was on a Monday and they were to use one of the rooms in the church.

When the appointed day came, they all gathered in the room. After a short exhortation, Bro. Jonah began to rebuke the devil openly. The reaction was immediate. The drama members began to manifest; some fell under the power of God, while some were screaming and rolling on the floor. The commotion drew the attention of some of the church leaders who were in the premises. They stormed into the room and stopped the prayer that was going on. The shook the people who were manifesting and forced them into consciousness. Such was the level of opposition that they faced in those days.[6]

> Those who did not believe in demonology or deliverance ridiculed the ministry. Some called us different names to discourage their members from coming. But funny, those who derided us came 'nicodemusly' to be ministered to when they couldn't handle the challenges in their lives. Interestingly, Dr Ibeneme will still give them attention and attend to them painstakingly. This is another lesson to learn from him.[7]

Sometimes, during the Friday preparatory meetings, the Faith Clinic ministers would report what people were saying about the ministry. Whilst they felt rather hurt and angered by the comments they had heard — "it's a false doctrine;" "there's no deliverance in the Bible;" "they are using *juju* power" etc. — Bro. Ibe will simply say, "Don't worry; they don't understand now. It will soon be clear to them what we are doing. We are not doing it behind closed doors."[8] With this attitude and response, the workers were encouraged to focus on the work and not mind the opposition of men or their some-times derogatory comments.

SCEPTICS

The approach of those who were simply sceptical was a little different. Many of those who doubted came close enough to investigate and scrutinise what was happening at the meetings. Many of them went back not only convinced of the authenticity of the ministry, but also convicted of their need for salvation. Mary Bello shares one instance:

> We had people who came to scrutinise what we were doing. They tried to explain it away or find fault. I remember a medical practitioner who came and said the reason why people are manifesting is that we were touching them in some sensitive spots in their body. She said that people's nervous system will react in certain ways when triggered by certain actions. This was the reason why they fell to the ground. Well, when she fell under the power of God, no one touched her![8]

Another doctor in Enugu was so inquisitive and full of doubt. He stood close to the team while they ministered. When people fell under the power, he would place his stethoscope on the hands of the ministers to check only-God-knows-what! When they washed their hands, he would take the water away in order to run some tests. He wanted to know if there was any scientific explanation for the people's reactions — anything other than the name of Jesus Christ.

Of course, the doctor did not find anything that justified the manifestations — nothing physical, that is. However, he found faith.

> That man was a member of the Rosicrucian Order. He surrendered his life (to Christ) that day. He took us to his house to show us where he used to consult and communicate with spirits.[10]

When Thomas saw and touched the nail-marks in Jesus' hands, he exclaimed "My Lord and my King!"[11] God will always reveal Himself to those who are truly seeking to encounter Him. He always did at Faith Clinic.

8

OUTSIDE MINISTRATIONS

Despite all the misunderstandings that the ministry faced and endured, Faith Clinic Nigeria Inc. continued to grow and have an impact in the lives of many. There is yet another arm of the ministry that spread the influence of Faith Clinic abroad: the *outside ministrations*.

We can actually view the Faith Clinic move as a three-pronged spiritual operation that did much damage to the kingdom of darkness. The first aspect of the ministry, which we have already considered, was the all-night meetings every Saturday in Ibadan. Secondly, there was the Bible School, the teaching arm of the ministry that ran concurrently with the main deliverance sessions. The third operation, which was very powerful indeed, was what the ministers simply called the "outside ministrations." This third feature of Faith Clinic, as we would see in this chapter, extended the impact of the ministry of Faith Clinic beyond the Ibadan epicentre.

At the peak of the Faith Clinic move, people came to Ibadan from far and wide. The stadium at Adamasingba was always packed with seekers from all over Nigeria, as well as some neighbouring countries. Whenever Bro. Ibe was in the meetings, he would always acknowledge those who came from outside Nigeria and pray for them specially. The question is: How did the reputation of Faith Clinic go well beyond the Ibadan region? Central to this explosion was the "outside ministrations."

From the inception of Faith Clinic, there was so much demand placed on the grace and unction upon the life of Dr. Ibeneme. Every now and again, Bro. Ibe got invited to minister in conferences, churches and other meetings. Despite the fact that a number of denominations were sceptical about Faith Clinic, and some spoke openly against Bro. Ibe and the practice of deliverance, many doors still opened for Bro. Ibe to preach the undiluted message of Christ. Everywhere he went, the results were the same: the works of the enemy were exposed and people were set free from long-term spiritual bondages.

FAITH CLINIC AND FULL GOSPEL

Particularly, God used the Full Gospel Business Men's Fellowship (FGBMF) to open up the nation to the ministry of Bro. Ibe, who was himself a member of the organisation. Pastor Alex Adegboye, who was once a president of the FGBMF in Ibadan, had previously met Bro. Ibe through his brother, Prof. Victor Adegboye, in the 1970s (Bro. Ibe and Prof. Adegboye were colleagues in medical school at the time). However, he became more acquainted with Bro. Ibe through the activities of the FGBMF.[1] Pastor Alex recalls Bro. Ibe's presence at the very first meeting that Full Gospel held in Ibadan.

> The Chapter had begun when some members from Port Harcourt organised the first meeting. People had invited their friends and colleagues to the meeting. Bro. Ibeneme was a part of this first meeting.[2]

While many church groups were grappling with what seemed like a new spiritual experience and somewhat controversial theological concept, why did the FGBMF readily embrace Faith Clinic and the ministry of Bro. Ibe? Pastor Alex offers some valuable insight:

> The ministry of deliverance, especially with the accompanying manifestations, was a new phenomenon at the time. It was not happening among the SU,[3] FCS,[4] SCM[5] or the CSSM.[6] However, although it was new, the FGBMF was able to embrace it because of the credibility of the principal player, Bro. Ibeneme. He was known to many of the leaders. They were comfortable with the fact that he was able to substantiate the ministry from the Scriptures. Although he was not part of the Exco, he usually attended the meetings.[7]

Pastor Alex admits further:

> Although I personally visited the meetings of Faith Clinic just once, as a result of the news that was making the rounds about the various manifestations and works of power that were going on there, I had personal contact with the servant of God that led the

movement... I also got more acquainted with the work (of Faith Clinic) because the FGBMF in the city of Ibadan rode on the crest of the ministry of Faith Clinic. We had common grounds in soul-winning, which was the primary focus of the FGBMF.[8]

The ministry of Faith Clinic complemented FGBMF perfectly. They both had a focus on salvation, and believed in healing, the baptism of the Holy Spirit with the evidence of speaking in tongues, and of course, the biblical concept of deliverance. The format of the Full Gospel meetings always involved the sharing of personal salvation stories, and Faith Clinic supplied many on a regular basis.

Pastor Alex was there the day Aunty Christie got born again (read full story in chapter 4). Her subsequent deliverance at Faith Clinic was a big testimony. She joined the FGBMF afterwards and gave her testimony in many meetings. According to Pastor Alex, "Her testimony was the hottest!"[9] Aunty Christie confirmed that she went virtually everywhere to share her testimony of salvation and deliverance, mostly in Full Gospel meetings and in the company of Bro. Ibe.[10]

This, then, was the open door for Bro. Ibe's "outside ministrations" (what I am calling the "third arm" of Faith Clinic's operations). From that time in 1985 and throughout the peak of the ministry, invitations for Bro. Ibe to minister in various meetings and cities kept on coming into the Faith Clinic office. Many of these meetings led to the birth of new Full Gospel chapters.

THE TRAVELLING TEAM

Bro. Ibe was passionate about setting captives free from spiritual bondage. He was evidently called and anointed for this ministry. With the knowledge that there would always be a need to minister deliverance to people wherever he was invited, Bro. Ibe rarely travelled alone. He always went with a team. Some of the people frequently travelled with were Rev. Yemi Ayodele, Bro. Okarter, Aunty Christie, Biodun Alimi, Marcus Benson, Chucks Amaefule, and many others.

The team travelled everywhere the Lord opened doors for the ministry — the north, east, south and west of Nigeria, almost all the major cities. They travelled long distances by road and sometimes by air. Everywhere they went, the story was the same — the authority of the believer over the devil and his cohorts was exhibited for all to see. Many got saved and even more got delivered from demonic oppression.

The team members did not only witness unusual manifestation of God's miraculous power, they also got to know Bro. Ibe from a closer range. Almost unanimously, their testimonies about the person of Bro. Ibe were the same; that Bro. Ibe was not only greatly anointed, but also a simple, approachable and loveable man of God. They all learnt different things from him during their travels.

Marcus Benson recalls vividly:

> Dr. Ibe was a giver. I discovered that Bro. Ibe was not in ministry because he wanted money. He did not care if he was given money for ministering or not. He only insisted on accommodation, and not

necessarily a hotel. It could be a member's house. Even when he was given an honorarium, he would share it with the ministers that accompanied him."[11]

Aunty Christie, during a Faith Clinic conference in 2010, talked about the light side of Bro. Ibe. She said the ministry team once gathered together to eat, and while a brother prayed over the food, Bro. Ibe took a piece of meat from everyone's plate![12] She also shared an incidence that happened during a trip to Togo:

> We were once invited to minister in Togo. On getting to the boarder, the officials asked us for a bribe but Bro. Ibe refused to give them anything. They decided to delay us. Instead of argue or fight, we danced and praised God for one hour, after which they let us go.[13]

Victor Amosun was the leader of the Bible School, but he also travelled with Bro. Ibe on a number of occasions. He recounts a particular incident that reveals the person of Bro. Ibe.

> I recall a time when we travelled for an outside ministration and the other team members had occupied the hotel rooms reserved for us. Without hesitation, Bro. Ibe went to sleep on a carton by the mai-gaurd (security man). When I saw him, I was shocked. I said to myself, "If my boss could sleep here, I better follow suit." I was deeply touched by this extent of humility. What a lesson for us in this generation![14]

Christopher Okarter travelled with Bro. Ibe a lot. He revealed that Bro. Ibe would always make sure that his team members were well catered for. He would not accept his own room allocation until everyone else in the team has been allocated their rooms.[15]

Bro. Okarter also shared a touching story about Bro. Ibe's disposition to love and unity. He recalled a time when two of the ministers in Faith Clinic, Sis. Lola Bello and Sis. Yemisi Akande, had a sharp disagreement. Prior to this time, they were the best of friends; they had a food business that they ran together. Along the line, something happened between them that they could not resolve, and as a result, they ceased relating with each other. Many of the ministers knew about the situation and tried to restore their friendship, but every attempt failed. The sisters stopped talking to each other and avoided one another by all means. The case resembled one that Paul documented in his letter to the Philippians:

> I beseech Euodias, and beseech Syntyche, that they be of the same mind in the Lord. And I intreat thee also, true yokefellow, help those women which laboured with me in the gospel with Clement also, and with other my fellowlabourers, whose names are in the book of life.[16]

Unfortunately, no amount of "beseeching" or "intreating" worked for these sisters!

During one of the Friday preparatory meetings, when the ministers would find out who would take what programme on Saturday, and who would accompany Bro. Ibe on the next outside ministration, everyone was shocked to find the names of the two sisters among those who would go with him to Enugu. They wondered why, knowing the wicked devices of satan, Bro. Ibe would take two warring parties to the battlefield of deliverance! They were all of the opinion that the strife between the sisters would expose them to the enemy's attacks.

Unsurprisingly, Sis. Lola and Sis. Yemisi sat at opposite ends of the vehicle and did not talk to each other throughout the journey. They arrived at the hotel and were given the room numbers that had been reserved for them. As usual, the ministers occupied rooms in pairs, and this time, Bro. Ibe was going to do the allocation. To the surprise of everyone, Bro. Ibe called out the names of the two sisters and gave them one room to share! The ministers looked at each other in utter amazement, but no one summoned the courage to make a comment or question their leader's wisdom.

Everyone went to their rooms to rest and prepare for the evening session. However, their minds were not on the ministry they had come for; they were waiting to hear the sound of commotion and fighting in the sisters' room! Well, they heard no such thing. Instead, when it was time for the meeting, they knocked on their door and were surprised to find both sisters sharing powder and chatting away as though nothing had ever happened between them! The wisdom and prayers of Bro. Ibe were effective after all! Both sisters are still very good friends till this day, even after starting families of their own.

Bro. Ibe would always look for a way to establish love and unity among the brethren, even when everyone else had given up—his life being an obvious example of sacrificial love.[17]

MIRACLES ON THE ROAD

Many of the outside ministrations started on a Friday with a teaching session, during which an altar call for salvation was made. On Saturday morning, there was teaching on deliverance—origin of demons; causes of demonic oppression; the victory that Jesus wrought for us on the cross etc. This session was also used to train and pray for mature believers in the church or region, who later joined the team to minister deliverance in the evening. Bro. Ibe was keen that such believers would be equipped to continue walking in their authority over the demonic long after they had gone. In this way, he made people aware that the grace to cast out devils did not belong to him and the Faith Clinic ministers alone, but to everyone who professes faith in the Lord Jesus Christ.

Needless to say, God confirmed the ministry of Bro. Ibe and the travelling team with signs, wonders, diverse miracles and the operations of the Holy Spirit. The same kind of results that were occurring at Faith Clinic Ibadan were also happening around the country as they ministered.

Remi Tejumola had the privilege of travelling with Bro. Ibe on some outside ministrations. He documented an experience in one of his blog posts.

> I was part of the Faith Clinic team that travelled with Dr. I. K. U. Ibeneme to minister at a camp-meeting, December 1985. It was a deliverance session with a church on the outskirt of Lagos State. Our method of ministry was to ask individuals what problem they have, and we minister accordingly.

After I had prayed with several people, it came to the turn of a brother. I went through the normal process of our ministration and he stuttered and said, "I am a stammerer." I was flabbergasted because at that moment I didn't know what to do. But I just said, "In Jesus' name, I plead the blood. Be healed!" and I took off to another place. During the testimony time, the brother said in very clear words, "You know me..." and the place became wild with excitement and shouts of "Hallelujah!" filled the air! He was healed. Glory be to God!

People get healed by the laying on of hands and also without it, but all in the name of Jesus![18]

Remi also shares another experience in his book, *The Holy Ghost Invasion:*

I was one of the four-man team that went with Reverend (Dr.) I.K.U. Ibeneme to minister at a church in Mushin, Lagos, in March 1986. He ministered on the first day, Friday, and left us there to continue till Sunday. On Saturday, there were just the four of us to minister to the whole church of well over a thousand people. We therefore asked for the assistance of the church workers.

When they came out, we decided to pray and lay hands on them so that the power of God would come upon them to assist us in the ministration. As we were laying hands on them one by one, I noticed that I was not feeling the anointing and it also seemed as if nothing was happening to those I was praying for. Suddenly, I noticed that one of them was doing his best to run away from my hands! I rushed to him and touched him on the head and bang! Down he went. I said to myself, "So the anointing is here!" Feelings can deceive you, but the Word of God is the truth.[19]

THE WICKED "SPIRIT-HUSBAND"

In the city of Kano, a woman heard Bro. Ibe's teaching on spiritual oppression and deliverance, and afterwards followed the team back to their hotel. She told Bro. Ibe that his message was a narrative of her life. She proceeded to share her sad story. On the day that her husband's family came to ask her hand in marriage, her uncle died. All the things they had bought for the wedding were used to bury the uncle. On the day of the wedding, her junior brother died. Everyone considered it a bad omen and an unfortunate coincidence. When she gave birth to her first son, another junior brother died. No one could understand or explain what was happening.

Another brother of hers was living with her and the husband at this time, and it happened that they had a slight disagreement. In the presence of the husband, this younger brother said angrily, "Don't think you can kill me like you killed the others. I am not going to die!"

On hearing this, the husband exclaimed, "No wonder! I have been thinking about it! These coincidences are becoming too coincidental! After you finish killing all the males in your family, you will then descend on me!" Spurred by this sudden enlightenment, he collected her wedding ring and the car he had given her, and sent her packing. She was devastated because, according to her, she had no hand in the death of her siblings.

The woman cried all the way to her family. They, in turn, went to consult their oracles and were told that she was the one responsible for the deaths in the family. Her husband's family also consulted their own oracles, and were told the same thing. So, rejected by her husband and her own family, she rented an apartment and began to live alone with her child.

The lady's husband met someone else and was planning to get married again. He gave the new woman the car that once belonged to his ex-wife. Two weeks before the date of the wedding, the new lady had an accident with the car and died. Perplexed, the husband came to her and said, "You don't want me to marry again, do you? Never mind, I will not marry any longer. From now on I will remain single. Just leave me alone in peace!"

"Doctor," the woman asked Bro. Ibe, tears already filling her eyes, "can I be this wicked and I don't even know it?"

"No, you are not wicked," Bro. Ibe assured her. "But there is a spirit that is doing this havoc in your life. Since this spirit is residing in you, when your people consulted their gods, it was your picture that they saw."

"If it is in me," she began to cry, "please take it away! Let it go!"

Bro. Ibe and the team led her to Christ in the hotel room and began to minister deliverance to her. With authority, they ordered the spirit that was tormenting her: "You spiritual husband that is disturbing this woman, I command you, come out in Jesus' name!"

The reaction was immediate. The once quiet, soft-spoken woman became wild and began to speak with a male's voice: "Haven't you heard my story? Haven't you heard how many people I have strangled? You can't cast me out!"

"You must come out in Jesus' name," Bro. Ibe insisted.

"Don't you know me?" the spirit asked, the woman's eyebrows raised slightly.

"Who are you?" Bro. demanded.

"I am *omo nkoku*; I am the *alewi lese*. I am the one who does what he says he will do!" the spirit retorted, giving its assumed names in the native Igbo and Yoruba languages.

"No you are not!" Bro. Ibe replied. "There is only one *Omo Nkoku*. There is only one *Alewi lese*. There is only One who does what He says He will do. His name is Jesus Christ the Lord!"

At this, the woman used her fingers to block her ears and the spirit screamed, "Don't call that name! Don't call that name! He is my greatest enemy! I do not want to hear that name!"

Bro. Ibe said, "I will not only call that name, but you will also call Him with your mouth!"

"N-o-o-o-o!" the spirit shouted. "I will not call that name! He is my greatest enemy! I will not call that name!" The woman jumped on the table, then the chair, then the bed, as though she was running from something.

The team intensified their prayers and ordered the spirit to confess the name of Jesus. Finally, the spirit said, "J-e-e-e-e-e-s-s-s-u-u-u-s-s!" As the words came out of the woman's mouth, she fell to the floor, the demon left and she was gloriously delivered. Halleluyah![20]

APPARITIONS IN OWERRI

Bro. Ibe was invited to the city of Owerri to minister, and as usual, he went with a team from Faith Clinic. Some weeks before this engagement, Bro. Ibe had heard reports of a woman who usually experienced some strange things in her body every Easter. During this religious festive period, she will suddenly find wounds on her palms, feet and side — in the exact places where the crucifixion marks of Jesus was. She would not only have these marks, but blood would also ooze out of them throughout the Easter holidays. She would go into trances and see visions. All these unusual events attracted spectators from across the city, who considered them signs from God.

The woman, however, had no control over these apparitions; and despite their spectacular nature, she had no inner peace at all.

The ministry of Bro. Ibe and the Faith Clinic team happened to be shortly after Easter. One of the people who came to Bro. Ibe for prayer had bandages on her hands. She shared with Bro. Ibe that she always had apparitions during Easter and could not restrain herself from seeing strange sights. Bro. Ibe realised that this was the woman he had heard about and proceeded to minister to her. She was set free from the spiritual bondage that she was in and her wounds healed up within two weeks. That was also the last time she had those eerie experiences.[21]

OVERWHELMED IN LAGOS

1n 1988, Bro. Ibe was invited to speak at the Full Gospel national convention in Lagos. It was a five-day programme to be held at the National Arts Theatre; a big event that attracted all the Full Gospel chapters nation-wide. As one of the guest speakers, Bro. Ibe was invited to give a talk on deliverance.

Bro. Ibe told the organising committee that there was no way he would speak about deliverance that there would not be demonic manifestations, and for this reason, he never travelled alone. He requested for the accommodation arrangements of his ministry team of five to seven people. The organisers, however, declined his request. They claimed that there was no provision in the programme for the kind of ministrations that were the norm at Faith Clinic. The organisers just wanted Bro. Ibe to give a talk within a stipulated amount of time. The programme was that regimented.

As a Full Gospel member himself, Bro. Ibe could not turn down the invitation for this inflexibility. However, judging better, he asked some of the Faith Clinic ministers to come on their own and make separate accommodation arrangements. Those who attended the event included Christopher Okarter, Aunty Christie, Biodun Alimi, Sis. Obi, Sis. Aderemi and others. They all went for the event and made individual bookings at the hotel. They also told Bro. Ibe jokingly, "When it all happens and you call us to come and minister to the people, we will not answer o! since they said they do not want deliverance."

On getting to the meeting, Bro. Ibe took his session within the time he was allocated. However, when he made an altar call at the end of his message, almost 85% of the crowd responded! The simple message that Bro. Ibe shared opened their eyes to the root of their problems.

Bro. Ibe prayed with those who were not yet saved. He then led them all in a corporate prayer to renounce their sinful or occultic past. Before you knew what was happening, people were falling under the anointing and demons were manifesting all over the place!

"Where is Bro. Okarter? Where is Biodun? Sis. Aderemi! Come and join me in the front of the hall!" Bro. Ibe began to call for his team of ministers over the public address system. They all came to the front and began to minister to the people that were manifesting.

The organisers announced that it was time for the next minister to come up stage, so those who were being prayed for were taken to the lobby of the National Arts Theatre. The need for ministry was so overwhelming, but God was not yet finished with His plan to take over the meeting.

One of the ministers[22] laid hands on a woman and she began to manifest violently. He tried his best to restrain her and then, leaving her on the floor, went on to lay hands on the person beside her. After a short while, the woman on the floor began to scream as if she was in some kind of agony, and to everyone's surprise, she vomited a baby lizard! Her teeth nearly caught the lizard's waist as it was coming out of her mouth! Subsequently, her eyes opened, the screams ceased, and she was wonderfully delivered!

The sight of the baby lizard astounded the woman and the minister who laid hands on her. Both of them, and everyone around could not believe their eyes. So, he paused and asked the lady for her story.

The woman was a widow who had come from the Eastern part of Nigeria. After the death of her husband, she began to feel strange movements in her body. Wherever the movements stopped momentarily, the place would swell and she would experience unbearable pain. If the swelling was on her arm, she would not be able to use it until the movements started again and moved to another part of her body.

She went to the Queen Elizabeth Hospital, Umuaha, where she worked as a nurse, for a medical check-up. But none of the tests revealed that anything was wrong with her. Seeing how discomforted she was, the doctor referred her to the University of Nigeria Teaching Hospital (UNTH) for further tests.

At UNTH, the diagnosis was the same. Thinking that she only needed a break from work, the consultant offered to give her a long-term sick leave, which she promptly declined. "I am dying of pain!" she complained bitterly. "Can't you see? Please do something to take this pain away!" she cried bitterly.

The consultant then referred her to the Lagos University Teaching Hospital (LUTH). This was why she had come to Lagos. Unknown to her, God had a miracle waiting for her because the friend she put up with happened to be a Full Gospel member. The day she came back from LUTH, her friend was on her way to the convention and she had no choice but to follow her. "Now see what the Lord has done!" she said with exceeding joy.

Bro. Ibe took the baby lizard to the main meeting and the woman shared her testimony. Needless to say, that was the end of the meeting as planned by the organisers! The remaining days of the convention was deliverance galore!

"We were arrested," shares Bro. Okarter, "and could no longer partake of the convention." The team was relocated to the Eko Meridian Hotel and the people who needed deliverance bombarded the hotel. The numbers were just too many for them to handle.

> I understood that day what it means for one's brain to 'knock' or 'snap'. I had talked and prayed so much that I could no longer hear myself as I spoke. It felt as if my brain had dried up! People surrounded us everywhere, wanting to be prayed for. The manifestations and deliverances were too much to recollect. Whenever we thought that we had finished ministering to the people, another set would appear because those who were being delivered had gone to bring their family members for ministry![23]

THE LAWFUL CAPTIVE IN ENUGU

Bro. Ibe and his team made a number of ministry trips to the city of Enugu. During one of these, they encountered a woman who had a peculiar need. The story of her deliverance depicts the kind of selflessness that the Faith Clinic minsters exhibited, obviously inspired by the character of their leader. It also contains many lessons for those who will be used of God today.

The lady, Chinedum, had very wealthy parents. Growing up in the midst of affluence, she became a highly-placed woman in society, had a very strong personality and was in control of much power. In spite of all these, she was battling with severe problems, not the least difficulties in finding a husband she could settle down with.

In search for lasting relief, she visited many prayer houses. A friend invited her to a particular "church" to see a certain "man-of-God." On getting there, she met a lot of people waiting to be called in to see the prophet. They had already been given numbers to indicate their turn in the queue.

All of a sudden, the man, Eddie, who was in an inner room, asked his aides to call her in. He described her to them and asked her to be brought in to his counselling room. He had not even seen her physically, neither was it yet her turn. Somehow, he had discerned her in the spirit and sought to enter into covenant with her.

Eddie, the so-called man-of-God, in the guise of helping to solve her problems, took her to a certain spot on top of a mountain, made some incantations and out came a large python. The snake opened its mouth and vomited a diamond. Eddie went on to cut the woman's finger nails; he cut her hair, the hair under her armpit and got some from her pubic area; he put them all together with the diamond and a piece of her clothing, and buried them by a tree on the mountain.

From that moment onwards, Chinedum came under Eddie's control. Her life was virtually at his mercy. Whatever Eddie demanded from her, he would get, almost at the snap of a finger. Whenever he needed to have her, no matter what time in the night, Chinedum would drive all the way to see him. Needless to say, her life went from bad to worse.

A friend had invited Chinedum to the meeting to see Bro. Ibe. However, the moment she came close to him, she ran back and people had to run after her. She could not even look at Bro. Ibe's face. She began to manifest even before the meeting started! Bro. Ibe and the team ministered to her patiently; they led her to Christ and broke every tie she had with spiritual entities in the spirit. This was the beginning of her long-drawn deliverance.

The spiritual influence that Eddie had on Chinedum was still very strong, and because she did not yet know the Word of God adequately, she kept on falling back into his hands. Soon after she left the meetings and the team had left town, Eddie's hold on her was reinforced.

False prophet Eddie told her that she was wasting her time going for deliverance, because she was his wife in the spirit. He also threatened to harm Bro. Ibe and warned the team to leave Chinedum alone. There was a time the team was ministering in Port Harcourt and Chinedum also travelled down for the meeting. As they ministered to her, the spirit in her began to speak: "You know since the day these people took you from me, I have not drank any blood. I am thirsty. Let me suck; let me suck." All of a sudden, Chinedum grabbed one of her breasts and began to scream. Soon afterwards, there were teeth marks on one of her breasts and she began to turn pale. There were times when they ministered to her that blood would begin to ooze out of her fingernails. Such was the depth of bondage she was in with this wicked spirit.

After one of their ministrations in Enugu, the team travelled back to Ibadan. Wanting to be sure that they had a safe trip, Chinedum called the Faith Clinic office the following morning and Bro. Okarter, who happened to be in the office at the time, picked the phone. In the middle of the call, the lady's voice suddenly turned into a man's voice. The spirit that manifested began to speak:

"I have warned you to leave Chinedum for me. There is nothing you can do to deliver her from my hands. Her life is in my control. In her wardrobe, there is a bottle with which I monitor her life. Back off, and don't waste your time!"

It was the spirit of the false prophet speaking through her. Obviously, Chinedum had no knowledge of what had come out of her mouth. Bro. Okarter straightaway informed Bro. Ibe of the strange thing he had heard, and told him he would go back to Enugu to deal with the matter and retrieve the bottle. Bro. Ibe prayed with him and sent him on his way.

Arriving at Enugu, Bro. Okarter went to the Faith Clinic ministry associates, the Nwosu's, and got a sister to accompany him on the rescue mission. Upon, seeing him, Chinedum enquired if everything was okay.

"All is well," Bro. Okarter replied. "The reason we came is to collect the bottle that is in your cupboard, the one that you talked about over the phone."

"Oh, the bottle?" she asked. "When you left the other day, I called pastors from the Grace of God Mission. They came and prayed for me. They have removed all the items I use for burning incense; they have also taken the bottle..."

As she continued speaking, the Holy Spirit told Bro. Okarter that it was a lying spirit impersonating itself as Chinedum. Just then, the phone rang, and Chinedum went to answer it.

Bro. Okarter, who had obviously prepared himself in prayer and fasting, went straight into Chinedum's room and found the bottle in her wardrobe. Meanwhile, they realised it was Eddie on the telephone with Chinedum. He was aware that the Faith Clinic ministers were around and what they had come for. He warned Chinedum sternly not to give them the bottle. But it was too late; they already had it in their possession.

When Chinedum came back into the room and saw the bottle in Bro. Okarter's hands, her countenance changed. "From now on," she began to rant, "I don't want to see you or Bro. Ibe again. I don't want your prayers. Just leave me alone!"

Full of boldness in the Holy Spirit, Bro. Okarter replied: "I came prepared for you, both spiritually and physically." He gave the bottle to the sister and she kept it in her handbag. They then began to pray in the spirit, binding and destroying every demonic influence controlling Chinedum's life.

After a while, Chinedum who had become hostile, suddenly changed, like someone waking up from sleep. She began to denounce her relationship with Eddie. "What good has he been to me? Why am I still following this man?" She then led the ministers to her bedroom and brought out all manners of items Eddie had given her, including black soaps, perfumes, creams, sponges and incense. Everything that she used for bathing and make-up were supplied to her by Eddie! Bro. Okarter packed three big nylon bags full of stuff back to Ibadan that day. These were items that Eddie used to exert control over her. On getting to Ibadan, Bro. Okarter showed Bro. Ibe the items. They prayed, broke the bottle and burned all the demonic items.

Strangely, soon after Bro. Okarter had left, there was a knock on Chinedum's gate. The gateman informed her that it was a lady whom he could not recognise. Chinedum allowed her in, entertained her and listened to the reason why she had come.

Chinedum eventually finished with the lady and as she was seeing her off down the stairs, she hit her feet on an imaginary stone and fell. By the time she managed to get up, she could not see the woman any longer. When she asked the gateman where the lady had gone, he had a quizzical look on his face because according to him, the lady was still with her in the house. Evidently, it was the false prophet who had come to draw her back in the spirit. Afterwards, he was able to hypnotise her and perform yet another terrible covenant ritual with her by a lake. He pronounced her his third wife in the spirit.

There was a further twist to her story before her complete deliverance. Bro. Ibe was back in Enugu for an outside ministration with the Full Gospel. As usual, they made contact with Chinedum just to find out how she was doing. On getting to the hotel that was reserved for them, they went through their usual process of room allocation. Bro. Ibe's room was an executive suite with a sitting area separate from the bedroom. The sitting room had a large settee.

For no apparent reason and quite uncharacteristically of him, Bro. Okarter chose to stay in Bro. Ibe's room. Every attempt to convince him to take the room reserved for him failed. "Why waste the money?" he asked. "Get a refund. The settee is big enough for me." Not able to convince him otherwise, Bro. Ibe consented.

Later that Friday night, after the ministration, they all retired to their rooms. Bro. Ibe, who was quite exhausted, slept off the moment he got on the bed. By a quarter to midnight, there was a knock on Bro. Ibe's door. Not knowing who it was or why Bro. Ibe was being sought after by that time of the night, Bro. Okarter opened the door, only to find Chinedum and another woman asking for Bro. Ibe. He wondered why they came that late and concluded it must be an emergency.

Bro. Ibe woke up and the two women entered the bed-room to chat with him. Bro. Okarter, discerning that they were in the middle of warfare, kept the adjoining door open and stayed awake all night, praying and checking constantly on them. By 2.00am in the morning, Bro. Okarter entered the room and the three of them had slept off on their chairs! When he woke them up, the women said it was too late for them to go back home. They stayed the night in the sitting room, but Bro. Okarter watched over Bro. Ibe till day break.

It was after her deliverance that Chinedum shared what happened that night. The false prophet and his cohorts had specially prepared her and the accomplice with a series of spiritual baths. They were both on a mission to weaken Bro. Ibe in the spirit. She confessed that, if need be, they were ready to cut off his private part! Thank God that their mission failed because of the eyes of the Lord that constantly watches over His own!

The final deliverance was also unusual. Bro. Ibe and the team were back in Enugu for a Full Gospel programme. They were lodged at the quarters of the Nigerian Cement Company. Bro. Ibe was in chalet no. 136 and Bro. Okarter was in no. 137. As it happened quite often, a couple was in Bro. Ibe's chalet discussing their infertility problems and other spiritual matters. Suddenly, Bro. Okarter noticed Chinedum driving into the compound. She was looking very rough, troubled and unhappy.

She went in to see Bro. Ibe, and after a while, Bro. Ibe asked Bro. Okarter to lead a team in praying for her. The moment he laid hands on her, she fell under the power and began to manifest. Unlike the normal shouts that people made, Chinedum was groaning like a woman in labour. She then began to strip herself, at which point Bro. Okarter called for Bro. Ibe through the intercom and asked him to come immediately.

Chinedum continued to writhe and scream in acute pain, like a woman in labour. As the demons were being expelled, she kept on screaming and pushing. All of a sudden, a still-born fish came out of her! Seven of them came out in the same manner and she was completely free.

Glory to God for his awesome power![24]

* * *

Chinedum's story shows the extent of spiritual bondage that many who patronise self-styled prayer houses and purported prophets can get themselves into. It unveils the nasty consequences of evil covenants made with the spirit realm, either wilfully or unknowingly. It reveals the extent to which the Faith Clinic ministers went at times to snatch some out of fire by all means. Most of all, it exalts Christ as the Lord and Mighty Deliverer. Chinedum was a lawful captive, but according to Scripture, even the lawful captives will be set free by the power in the blood of Jesus![25]

9

OVERFLOWING GLORY!

Whenever there is a sustained revival in a region or through a people united in faith and spirit, the presence of God comes to tabernacle over the area. The glory of heaven seems closer to the earth. The atmosphere of the region is charged with the power of God and there are many glorious signs and wonders during this time. Moreover, there is an abundance of open revelations and divine encounters with God, both during and after, inside and outside organised meetings. This has been the case in past revivals. It was certainly the norm during the Faith Clinic era. The glory that rested upon Faith Clinic in Ibadan expanded in ever-widening circles of divine activity across the nation and beyond.

Remi Tejumola shared a story that shows how dynamic the spiritual atmosphere and experiences at Faith Clinic were. A lady who had recently got born-again, and who lived in Jos, was having a lot of problems. She was also enduring much affliction and persecution from her family. One day, she had a revelation in which she was instructed to come to a place called Faith Clinic in Ibadan, over 900 kilometres south of Jos. Somehow, she had the feeling that if she did not locate this place called Faith Clinic, she would not be alive by the end of the week. The following day she travelled down to Ibadan and asking around for where she could locate Faith Clinic, she was directed to the office at House 5. It was a Tuesday.

Remi was in the office when she arrived. He counselled with her at length and since the main Faith Clinic ministrations were conducted in the weekend, he had asked her to find somewhere to stay till then (they rarely did any deliverance ministration during the week). As the woman turned to leave, he had a strong feeling to ask her to visit the Faith Clinic site and be ministered to straightaway. He himself went to the site and was joined by Aunty Christie in order to pray with her.

They started by ministering the baptism in the Holy Spirit to her. The moment they started praying, a demon manifested and said, "You are going to have a hard time casting me out today!"

It ended up being, in Remi's words, "one of the easiest deliverances I had conducted."[1] Not only was she gloriously delivered, she also received the baptism in the Holy Spirit with the evidence of speaking in tongues. In addition, she began to manifest the gifts of the Spirit in an unusual way. All the gifts were operating in her with much accuracy! The Lord began to speak through her about her life, her future and her ministry. By the word of knowledge, the Lord said her ministry was starting that very day!

Remi recalls his reaction:

> In my heart, I began to tell the Lord that I wanted to manifest the gifts of the Spirit in a similar way. The thought had not finished forming in my mind when the Lord, through this lady, began to speak to me. He said, "But you asked this morning to be used by me; I will yet use you beyond what you can presently conceive in your mind..." I was shocked! I knew the Lord heard my unexpressed words. I knelt down and she prayed for and prophesied over me. When she laid hands on Aunty Christie, she (Aunty Christie) got slain in the Holy Spirit![2]

Such was the glory that was manifesting in those days. Faith Clinic Ibadan was a power hub that transmitted the power of God across the nation. Many came under its influence and had life-changing encounters with heavens glory.

This heavenly glory brought with it the revelation about the believers' authority over the demonic realms. The attending manifestations were signs that caught the attention of believers everywhere. Before long, the same results were occurring in the lives of many.

God never meant for the revival to be restricted to a single location. The glory was never intended to be monopolised by a single person, present in a particular ministry or confined to a weekend meeting. The signs of healing and the casting out of devils were to follow believers everywhere they went. God used the ministry of Faith Clinic to restore this spiritual reality to the Church in Nigeria in a very powerful way.

Bro. Ibe also had this viewpoint. This is why Faith Clinic remained a para-church ministry throughout the revival period.[3] The vision was for believers to receive deliverance, get filled with the Spirit, be equipped in the word, and thereafter go forth as ambassadors of Christ, manifesting the same glory everywhere. It is not possible to quantify the influence that Faith Clinic had over a generation of people, especially youngsters who were hungry for God.

MANIFESTATIONS IN QUEEN'S SCHOOL

My cousin, Ope Nubi,[4] had become born again in 1984, her final secondary school year in Queen's School, Ibadan. She started A' Levels the following year and was a boarding house student. During fellowship times at the boarding house, the students, who were in their teens, began to witness some unusual and dramatic manifestations when they gathered together. Some would fall under the power and start rolling on the floor. Others would run out of the charged atmosphere and the demons in them would start screaming hysterically.

God began to tutor and guide Ope and her friends in the art of spiritual warfare and on how to exercise dominion over demons in the name of Jesus. It was no surprise, then, when she attended Faith Clinic for the first time in 1985 and saw the same kind of manifestations there. From that first time, she attended often and experienced rapid growth in her walk with God.[5]

A year later, in August 1986, during her father's 50th birthday, Ope spent hours telling me many exciting things that were happening in her school; how demons were manifesting in young girls and how they learnt to cast them out. These were thrilling encounters that would catch the attention of any teenager.

Lying on my bed early the following morning, with thoughts of my cousin and her stories still fresh on my mind, I came under the conviction of the Holy Spirit. I did not yet know first-hand the Person Ope knew. Right there on my bed, with no one present but the Holy Spirit, I gave my life to Christ and rose up a new person! The following morning, I received the gift to write and had an unusual experience of my own: I wrote non-stop for nineteen hours many prophetic things about the last days! I have continued writing ever since.

Thankfully, I am a direct beneficiary of the abiding glory that permeated the Ibadan region in the 1980s, Faith Clinic being a focal point. This same glory has transformed the lives of untold numbers of people, both young and old.

UNIVERSITY STUDENTS

Alric Niyi Amona was a student at the Ogun State University in Ago Iwoye[6] in the eighties. He was already a believer who was passionate about the things of God. Coming in contact with Faith Clinic increased his spiritual hunger many times over. He frequented the meetings whilst still a student and saw the power of God in action. The things he witnessed made him believe that God's power is real and his calling into the ministry is worth embracing. Today, he leads a thriving church in

Ibadan and is used of God to conduct mass evangelistic campaigns.[7]

Lanre Jegede was a student in the University of Ibadan during the revival. He was known on campus as "that Faith Clinic brother" because he always attended the prayer meetings on Friday and the programme on Saturday.[8] Today he leads a network of churches in the United Kingdom. Without a doubt, there are hundreds more like him dotted all over the nation and beyond.

REVIVAL IN FELELE

My father, late Kunle Odulaja of blessed memory, was a committed minister at Faith Clinic. Prior to his joining Faith Clinic in 1986, he had been a typical sinner – a chain -smoker, an alcoholic, a gambler and a womaniser. Some months before he came across Faith Clinic, my father had met with God and experienced a drastic turnaround in his life. His association with Faith Clinic turned him into a firebrand who carried the power and grace of God everywhere he went.

The Faith Clinic revival spread through my father to the local church that our family attended at the time, New Salem Church, Felele branch.[9] Soon, demons where manifesting in people considered to be "nice" Christians, including deacons and church workers! The manifestations caused some to react in criticism, but the pastor of the church, Apostle J.D. Adefenwa, wisely created a space away from the church for fellowship and deliverance meetings. Every week, we held services that were patterned after the Faith Clinic format. We had the first message (salvation), testimonies, healing, deliverance and the baptism of the Holy Spirit! The only difference was that it was an evening meeting and not an all-night service. The manifestations and testimonies were the same as those happening at Faith Clinic.[10]

When my father moved to Ijebu-Ode, he continued to spread the message and glory of Christ, with signs following. Again, eternity will reveal the number of people who because of the move of God at Faith Clinic, manifested the glory of God and touched lives in their own sphere of influence.

THE GLORY TOUCHES THE ANGLICAN CHURCH

We have seen how the Full Gospel Business Men's Fellowship was instrumental in opening doors for Faith Clinic around the country. The surprising truth is that the Anglican church was equally receptive to the ministry of Bro. Ibe. A good number of the "outside ministrations" were due to the invitations of Anglican Church parishes. They were one of the first church groups to recognise the need for deliverance, and gradually embrace the ministry of Faith Clinic and Bro. Ibe.

Many of the vicars and church leaders were actually involved in the occult at the time (and this was common knowledge), however a few of them, including some influential members were saved and were also members of the FGBMF. It was these ones that God used to prevail over the authorities to invite Bro. Ibe to minister from time to time. And he readily obliged.

Bro. Ibe was a non-denominational minister who considered himself a servant of the entire body and not just a sub-section of it. The Anglican parishes invited Bro. Ibe for healing meetings, revivals or crusades, but they always got more than they bargained for. The opportunity to minister always proved crucial and effective.

Bro. Ibe was once invited to the All Saints' Cathedral in Enugu. The meeting was so powerful that people still refer to it today. Many souls gave their lives to Christ after hearing the word of God. Bro. Ibeneme had preached about occultism in the church and what the devil was doing to oppress ignorant believers. Of course, the people knew that there were members of the Ogboni fraternity and the Rosicrucian Society in the church. It was acceptable in those days. At times, the church vestry was used for initiation ceremonies. Many newly formed Pentecostal and Charismatic churches decried the situation from afar and referred to the Anglican Church as "dead" in religion. But God gave Bro. Ibe grace to engage the situation with the word and power of God.

After the teaching at this Anglican Church, the organist of the church, who was one of the assistant priests, got convicted by the message. He came to see Bro. Ibe in his hotel room and confessed that he was a member of the Lodge (since Bro. Ibe had spoken against it). He wanted to know if what Bro. had preached about was really true.

"Does it mean that if I continue as a Lodge member, I am bound to go to hell?" he had asked.

"Unfortunately, yes," Bro. Ibe had told him, making reference to the Scriptures.

After hearing what Bro. Ibe had to say, the man was ready to renounce his Lodge membership and receive Christ as his Lord and Saviour. The team gladly led him in the sinner's prayer.

After the prayer, the man pledged to bring all the items and instruments that connected him to the Lodge. And he did. He brought the box that contained his Lodge regalia, his sword and other items; he handed them over to Bro. Ibe, who prayed with him, and encouraged him to stand fast in the faith.

With joy in his heart, the church organist went to the church vicar and told him about his decision to leave the Lodge and follow Christ wholeheartedly. Instead of rejoice with him, the vicar, together with the rest of the church leadership, rose up against him. They put pressure on him to collect the items back, and threatened to excommunicate him from the church if he did not do so. Confused and terrified, he came back to Bro. Ibe and begged to receive the items back. This just shows how ingrained the problem of occultism was in the church back then. Notwithstanding, Bro. Ibe and his "outside ministration" team kept on honouring invitations to the Anglican Church. With persistence over the revival years, many people received Christ, got delivered and were baptised in the Holy Spirit.

The fruit of Bro. Ibe's tireless labour among the Anglican Churches is now evident. Majority of the vicars are now born again and open to the operations of the Spirit. Just a few years ago, the new leader of the Church, Rev. J.O. Akinfenwa, when taking the oath of office, made an open declaration before the people. He swore before the Lord that he was not a member of any secret society and does not intend to join any. Afterwards, he lined up all the ministers of the church and got them to make the same confession in the name of the Lord.[11] Heaven alone knows how much of Bro. Ibe's sacrificial labours contributed to the dramatic turnaround of what was once labelled a "dead" Church. Jesus is truly the resurrection and the life!

THE MID-WEEK "FAITH CLINIC" LEGACY

We have already noted that before the Faith Clinic revival started in 1983, a practical knowledge of the believers' authority to cast out devils was almost non-existent in the Church. The reality and operations of evil spirits were also a mystery, as well as the roots of many problems people were facing. The revival brought all these to light. As more and more people passed through the abiding glory at Faith Clinic, they began to understand how to minister deliverance in the name of Jesus.

The Faith Clinic Bible School was instrumental in equipping hundreds of believers for the work of the ministry. Each graduating set of students was charged with the mandate to spread the knowledge of Christ and destroy the works of the devil everywhere they found themselves, especially in their local churches. In fact, the Faith Clinic teachers were frequently invited to train workers in different churches, while some churches sent groups of people to take the courses at Faith Clinic.

Moreover, as mentioned before, whenever Bro. Ibe and

the team went for outside ministrations, they always asked for the church or ministry's prayer team; they would minister to and pray with them; then get them to minister alongside them during the ministrations in the hope that they will gain some experience and continue the ministry after they had left.

The resultant effect of all these teachings and hands-on activities was that a practice that was once unknown or restricted in the churches soon became a widespread custom. Many churches began to set up deliverance teams that could counsel and pray for those who were experiencing any kind of oppression. Other churches, like the *Redeemed Christian Church of God*, added a "Faith Clinic" service to their mid-week programme, a time to deal with problematic situations through prayer and deliverance. This is a lasting legacy of a revival that was once misunderstood but greatly used of God amongst us.

A PLATFORM FOR GLORY

Bro. Ibe never saw himself as the only one anointed to minister deliverance. From the early days of Faith Clinic, he was committed to raising others who would be competent enough to do what he was anointed to do. He mentored many and became an exemplary leader to those around him. Apart from the Faith Clinic platform, which was effective in developing the gifting of emerging leaders, Bro. Ibe never shied away from exposing his disciples to ministry opportunities.

The commitment of Bro. Ibe to developing ministers was down to the fact that he was secure in his calling and anointing. He did not only take younger ministers with him for outside ministrations, he also took them along to see other senior ministers.

Mary Oluwatayo[12] was not even a Faith Clinic minister when she encountered Bro. Ibe for the first time; she was an active member of the choir of *Foursquare Gospel Church Headquarters* in Alagomeji, Yaba. He had come for an outside ministration and had also prayed for her. It was a brief meeting and Bro. Ibe had asked her to visit Faith Clinic whenever she had the chance. A few months later, she travelled to Ibadan and met with Bro. Ibe in his office. To her surprise, Bro. Ibe did not only recognise her, he asked her to accompany him and others to Benin City, to visit Archbishop Benson Idahosa! She was flabbergasted, to say the least. The three-day stay at Benson Idahosa's residence in 1984 has remained an unforgettable encounter in Mary's life.[13] Marcus Benson and a few others were also taken along on this trip, which reflects the heart Bro. Ibe had for exposing and raising others.[14]

Before long, Bro. Ibe was able to send out ministers to represent him in places that he could not attend. Marcus Benson remembers his ministerial development under Bro. Ibe quite vividly:

> It was through Dr. Ibe that I was able to see and fellowship with Archbishop Benson Idahosa, as well as Dr. Adeboye. Dr. Ibe was very open. He never went to these people alone; he always brought people along. Dr. Ibe was secure in himself.
>
> There was a time that he could not attend a meeting at Pentecostal Assembly Lagos. He sent a team,

including myself, to represent him. The meeting was so powerful and the news of the things that happened got to Dr. Ibe. When he saw me, he said jokingly, "Marcus, Marcus, the man of the hour!" From that time, Bro. Ibe sent more of us to represent him when he was not available to attend meetings. This was a form of training for us.

At another meeting, at the Foursquare Head-quarters, Bro. Ibe asked me to lead a team ahead of him. It was their convention. Bro. Ibe was to join us later in the meeting because he was going to drive from Ogbomosho. When he came, he sat in the crowd and listened as I spoke. Afterwards, he gave me feedback on the message I gave.[15]

EVER-INCREASING GLORY!

The following narrative of the experiences of Timothy Babatunde illustrates graphically how the glory of God that broke out in Faith Clinic flowed out in many directions. Timothy Babatunde was part of the leadership of WOSEM campus fellowship in University of Lagos. The fellowship had been going on for a few years. At some point in the early 1980s, they began to experience some unexplainable manifestations; incidents that they could not understand or handle. Some of the believers were manifesting demons, and the leadership did not know what to do. It was at this point that someone recommended that he visited somewhere in Ibadan called Faith Clinic.

The young Timothy travelled to Ibadan and attended a Faith Clinic meeting. At this first encounter, he witnessed things he had never seen before and was astonished. He saw people being delivered of evil spirits; he saw the power of God in action. This was the beginning of many weekly visits to Faith Clinic from Lagos.

Timothy was curious to know what was responsible for the power he was seeing at Faith Clinic. What was the secret? Were they into black magic? He decided to get close to the team and discover for himself.

Timothy began to arrive at Ibadan very early, long before the main meeting commenced at 7.30pm. He would go to the venue of the meeting at UCH to observe what happened before the meetings. Instead of discover anything untoward, he noticed that before each meeting, the Faith Clinic ministers engaged in powerful intercession. They would pray for hours and afterwards start the meetings. The resultant effect of their prayers was the same all the time: unusual manifestations of God's power and the deliverance of people from demonic oppression.

The kinds of manifestations he witnessed were uncommon. People brought mad people to the meetings and God delivered them. He remembers a two-year old that had a problem with his eyes. The eyes were crossed and his vision was impaired. Dr. Ibeneme laid hands on the boy and surprisingly, there was a manifestation. A demon was cast out and the boy was totally healed.

He also remembers times when people came to test the power of God. Once, a wizard had come to the meeting. Dr. Ibeneme had a word of knowledge and said if the man does not come out to confess, he may not go home that night. He came out and was delivered.

Timothy began to take teams of people to Faith Clinic every week and they later started deliverance meetings in the church and campus fellowship. He also invited Dr. Ibeneme to the campus fellowship and God's servant agreed to come.

The meeting at the WOSEM fellowship was remarkable. While Dr. Ibeneme was ministering God's word, two ladies were disturbing the service at the back of the hall. Dr. Ibeneme just continued sharing, ignoring their manifestations. After a while, they both left the hall. Moments later, Dr. Ibeneme announced that when he starts to pray for people, that the two girls will come back from wherever they went. "The power of God will bring them back," he had said confidently. And it happened just as he said. In a state of stupor, the two girls came back to the meeting when the power of God broke out, and they were gloriously delivered.

"The beautiful thing about the ministration," Timothy says, "was that every deliverance case was by the Word. Dr. Ibeneme was ministering with great authority and his word was filled with power."[16]

He continues his narrative:

> I was so moved by all the things I saw during this meeting that I travelled to Ibadan the next day to see Dr. Ibeneme. When I eventually got an audience with him, I expressed my wonder at the things I had seen the day before, and asked how can these things be? Dr. Ibeneme smiled and said to me: "It can happen through anyone. Just make yourself available to God."

Dr. Ibeneme was such a simple, approachable man. He was quite unusual, gentle and was obviously accustomed to fasting. To the eyes, it seemed he had the skin of a baby.

"We will like to have you back," I asked Dr. Ibeneme. However, the date I requested for was not convenient. "I do not have to be there in person," Dr. Ibeneme had said. "I will send someone to represent me."

When the day of the meeting came, Dr. Ibeneme's representative was very punctual. He arrived before many of the believers came, which gave me time to observe him before the meeting.

"Hello, my name is Biodun Alimi." I must confess, upon seeing the way he was dressed, I was not immediately impressed. How can Dr. Ibeneme send someone like him to stand in his place? Brother Alimi was dressed in a simple jeans and T-shirt, and was wearing a casual sandal. *What could he possibly do?* I thought.

My pastor introduced Brother Alimi, the preacher of the day. He probably had the same doubts that I had. "Well, over to you, Brother Alimi," the pastor had said.

When Brother Alimi took the microphone, he greeted the congregation and straightaway opened to a Scripture in Isaiah. He quoted it repeatedly for a while, and then turned his attention to the choir. At a command in the name of Jesus, demons began to manifest in many of the choristers! Many of them were crashing to the floor, screaming and throwing up stuff. The whole place was chaotic, to say the least.

After a while, he used the evidence of what had just happened to teach on the origin and mission of demons. He spoke confidently and authoritatively.

After the teaching, another chaotic session of expelling devils commenced. Long before this time in the service, I had repented of judging God's servant by his outward looks. We later became very good friends.[17]

Timothy's weekly visits to Faith Clinic continued. Also, both he and his team attended the Faith Clinic Bible School. He got close to Dr. Ibeneme and saw more of his humility and simplicity.

Dr. Ibeneme will spend time with all of the young ministers after ministrations. He'll joke with us and share stories about his walk with God. So much was learnt during these times.

God used Dr. Ibeneme to display and emphasise the authority of the believer in another dimension. Just by being around him, there was a transfer of anointing. His word of knowledge was accurate and the gifts of the Spirit were precise.

I knew about healing before coming in contact with Faith Clinic, but not deliverance. I had no knowledge of the process of casting out demons, apart from reading it in the Scriptures. Through Faith Clinic, deliverance from demonic strongholds became an experiential reality in my life and the church.[18]

Today, Timothy Babatunde leads a thriving church in Pennsylvania, USA. This is overflowing glory of untold dimensions!

MINISTRY REPLICATION IN ABA

The story of how God began to use Dr. Ogini, a gynaecologist based in Aba, to minister Christ to others is fascinating. Prior to encountering the Faith Clinic ministry, he was a stark unbeliever who did not believe in the supernatural. His wife and son would always attend Faith Clinic meetings whenever the team came to the East, but he would not have any of it. In fact, he often victimised his wife for going to fellowship, and would sometimes lock her out of the compound. "With all your learning and education," he would mock, "you sit down to listen to someone preach the Bible to you for hours!" All this sarcasm would soon change when he became paralysed on one side and needed the intervention of God.

A brother of one of the Faith Clinic ministers, who worked as a technician in the doctor's hospital, brought the situation to the minister's attention and pleaded with him to come and pray for his boss. It was at this meeting that the doctor narrated what had happened.

"I have never seen anything like this before!" the doctor began his story. "One of my patients, who was a few months pregnant, came to me one day with an unusual request: 'I want you to remove these babies from my womb; they are worrying me. I want to go home!'

"I asked her what she meant, and she said, 'My people

are calling me.' I then asked her, 'Who are your people?' Her strange reply was, 'They are under the water, and they want me to come home.'

"I thought she was just hallucinating because of the stress of her pregnancy. 'Madam, just go home and rest.' She insisted with her request. 'Look at your pregnancy; I can't operate on you now.' And in a bid to get rid of her, I added, 'Come back when the pregnancy is seven months and I will remove the babies for you.' At this, she got up and left.

"Exactly seven months into the pregnancy, the woman came back. She came with all her luggage and said to me, 'You are not leaving this hospital today until you operate on me and bring out these babies! They are disturbing me!'

"At this, I called the woman's husband and he confirmed that they have been fighting over the issue for months; that since this is what she wanted, I should go ahead with the operation. So, I did the surgery, removed the baby, and sewed her up. As I moved to the sink to wash my hands, I discovered I could not use my right hand. My right leg also became heavy. Thinking it was due to overwork, I managed to drag myself to the sink. As I picked up the soap, it fell off my hands. 'What is going on?' I had thought.

"I called my wife, who also worked with me in the hospital, and she came for me. By the time we got back home, I became completely paralysed on one side of my body. Doctors have conducted all manners of tests and they have not found anything abnormal with me. Please what is the meaning of all this?"

The minister told him, "Oga, before now, you did not believe in spiritual things. This is spiritual. The people from whom you rescued the pregnant woman are the ones afflicting you. Since you do not have Jesus in your life, their powers are prevailing over you. Will you accept Jesus as your Lord and Saviour? He will deliver you from this affliction and you will be well again."

Without any hesitation, the doctor accepted Christ into his life. Prior to this time, some friends had arranged for him to be admitted into a hospital in Canada. The hospital needed him to carry out some tests before his arrival, and since the equipment needed for the tests were not available in the East, he was scheduled to have them done in UCH, Ibadan.

"Fine," the minister said. "I will allow you to do all your medical findings so that when God does it, you will know it was the hand of God and not mere coincidence. When you finish at the hospital, I will take you to Faith Clinic. It is held in Ibadan on a Saturday night." They prayed together and left it at that.

The consultants at UCH ran about eight x-rays and tests, but could not find anything responsible for his condition. Afterwards, he came to Faith Clinic, at Adamasingba stadium. During the healing session, the doctor came out for prayers. The moment hands were laid on him, he fell to the ground. He began to scream, and his body was vibrating violently like a grinding machine. He went on like this for nearly an hour.

After the manifestation subsided, the doctor stood up from the floor. He was able to lift his hands, stretch his legs, touch his toes and run around! He was totally healed from the paralysis!

"What?" the doctor exclaimed. "You mean there is power like this in the name of Jesus?"

The doctor did not only repent of his sins of unbelief; when he got back home, he looked for the biggest Dake's Bible that he could find and began to carry it everywhere with him! "Do you know why I am carrying this big Bible?" he once asked the minister. "I want people who see it to ask me the same question, so I would have the opportunity to tell them my testimony."

Over time, God endowed the doctor with so much grace and unction, that when some of his patients came for treatment, the gifts of the Spirit would operate precisely through him and he would show them the root causes of their predicaments. In this way, he led many to Christ and was used to minister deliverance to the oppressed. He also ministered to all his workers and led them to Christ. The doctor later became one of the presidents of the Full Gospel Business Men's Fellowship, Aba chapter. Praise the name of the Lord forever more![19]

BEYOND THE NIGERIAN BORDERS

I have already hinted that the ministry of Faith Clinic touched lives outside the Nigerian federation; that many people came all the way to Ibadan to attend the all-night deliverance meetings. God actually opened some international doors for Bro. Ibe to preach and demonstrate the message of the believers authority over devils.

Bro. Ibe was invited to minister in Ghana in 1988. With him on this trip, amongst others, was Chucks Amaefule. So many awesome things happened during the ministry, including the miraculous healing of the wife of a former finance minister. Also, at one Calvary Baptist church, it was reported that the power of God was so heavy upon the meetings to the extent that people were falling under the power and manifesting a considerable radius outside the church! These ones were brought into the service and ministered to accordingly.

Later that year, the finance minister whose wife got healed invited Bro. Ibe to the United Kingdom. He had a grand reception for them at his residence in St. John's Wood. During this visit, Bro. Ibe, accompanied by Chucks Amaefule and Bro. Obaze, ministered in a number of churches, including Kensington Temple, led by Rev. Colin Dye. The glorious power of God to save and deliver was demonstrated in these meetings too.

The plan of the team was to move on to America from the UK, where some meetings had been arranged. However, for no apparent reason, the US Embassy declined their application for visas. Every attempt to rectify the situation failed, which was also surprising considering the high-level contacts that they had to give them assistance.

Well, thanks be to God who chose to close the door to the USA. If everything had gone to plan, the team would have travelled on the 21st of December, 1988, on the Pan Am Flight 103 that took off from Heathrow. Sadly, this flight never reached its destination, which was to be the John F. Kennedy International Airport, New York. The Boeing 747-

121 plane "was destroyed by an explosive device killing all 243 passengers and 16 crew members."[20] The incidence is popularly known as the Lockerbie bombing.[21]

Praise God for Him many deliverances!

* * *

It is not possible to write about all the awesome ways that the glory of God manifested beyond Faith Clinic, Ibadan. John was right when he considered the overwhelming task of writing all the miracles that Jesus did during His earthly ministry.[22] Thanks be to God, for heaven holds all the records!

10

A GENERAL'S EXIT

Throughout history, God had always used human vessels as catalysts of His glorious moves. Without revivalists, there has hardly been any revival. These are bearers of His message and carriers of His power. Through their knowledge of and walk with God, they do exploits, influence the sons of men and advance the cause of righteousness on the earth. They and their ministries are recognised in heaven and feared in hell. Though ranked highly in God's army, many become all things to all men, and are usually celebrated as "God's generals" retrospectively.[1]

Rev. (Dr.) Izuwanne Ibeneme perfectly fits the description of a general in God's army. He was a mighty instrument in the hands of God, one that was used to shape the spiritual destiny of an entire generation of saints. He discipled young ministers and influenced more established ones. Yet, he did not take honour upon himself.

Marcus Benson made the following comment about him:

> Whenever he was introduced as Rev. Dr. Ibeneme, he would correct the notion and say, "I am not a Reverend; I am a brother." We learnt from him that God anoints men and not titles. We were all brothers. After a while, Archbishop Benson Idahosa convinced him into getting ordained. This happened in Benin City.[2]

Even though the name "Bro. Ibe" stuck with him, there was no doubt about the position that he occupied in the spirit.

AN APOSTLE OF UNITY

Bro. Ibe was one of the pioneers of the Ibadan Unity Ministers' Forum — an accountability group of ministers who relate openly with one another. He was the first chairman of the group that included ministers like Rev. Bank Akinmola, Rev. Emiko Amotsuka, Pastor Alex Adegboye, Pastor Lekan Babatunde, and many others.[3] Bro. Ibe had a passion for oneness and openness in the Church, especially among leaders. He related with ministers and ministries across the city and nation. Whenever there was any conflict among ministers, he did all that he could to resolve the conflict and restore peace. He had an understanding of the Body of Christ and strove to maintain unity among the ranks. He did not consider Faith Clinic an exclusive entity or set out to build an empire around himself. Instead, he made himself available to serve the household of God.

Faith Clinic in Ibadan became a platform for some of the ministers with whom Bro. Ibe related closely. None of them had a this-is-my-ministry attitude. Rev. Yemi Ayodele and Pastor Lekan Babatunde were some of his ministry colleagues during the revival. They were united in spirit and purpose. Chris Asudemade, one of the Faith Clinic ministers and, at the time, a member of *Jesus is King*, led by Pastor Lekan Babatunde, commented that many times Bro. Ibe would teach something at Faith Clinic, only for him to get to church and hear Pastor Lekan share the same thing. Such was the sense of unity among the ministers in those days. They were also all interested in mentoring and raising up the younger generation.[4]

Another written account by Akinwale Johnson, a Pastor with the New Covenant Church in Ilorin, depicts the spirit of oneness amongst the ministers and their heart for equipping the younger generation:

I learnt about Faith Clinic ministry under the leadership of late Rev. (Dr.) I.K.U. Ibeneme, around 1987. I attended the Bible school and became a Christian worker (minister) there. My areas of ministration there was salvation message and healing.

I continued to serve the Lord during my National Youth Service Corps (NYSC) in Kano state in 1991. I was the Evangelism Secretary in Nigeria Christian Corpers' Fellowship (NCCF), Kano State. It was during my youth service that God told me in a vision that I should invest all that He has blessed me with in the spread of the gospel. God said if I gave my whole lifetime in service to him, He would take care of me. He gave me a lot of revelations, and confirmed that He primarily made me to serve in His vineyard.

I decided to travel back to Ibadan to see my leader, late Rev (Dr.) I.K.U. Ibeneme, for further counsel; after all, in the multitude of counsel, there is safety. When I arrived Ibadan, I went straight to the Faith Clinic premises and discovered that they were having a special programme. They had invited Rev. Emmanuel Kure (a minister with prophetic gifting) from Kafanchan, Kaduna State to minister. He announced that day (Friday evening) that God had instructed him to pray with all workers (ministers) of Faith Clinic the following morning, which was Saturday. I attended the Saturday morning meeting and after sharing the word, he prayed with us individually and prophesied. I was the fourth person he prayed for and he said these about me... "The Spirit of God says expressly that you will be involved in ministry work at different levels. As an evangelist, you will preach and as a teacher, you will teach the word. The scriptures will come alive when you open it and you will teach men around you. You should be single-minded with your calling, not double-minded. You should work under men and not be independent..."

I had never met Rev. Emmanuel Kure before; I saw him for the first time the previous day, Friday, and he said those words under the influence of the

Holy Spirit. When I eventually met with Dr. I.K.U Ibeneme on Sunday evening, I told him that I purposely came to Ibadan on that trip to seek his fatherly, godly counsel regarding what I claimed God was telling me. The first question he asked me was whether I attended the workers' meeting with Emmanuel Kure. When I narrated what Rev. Kure said, he simply told me that was the confirmation to all that God had been telling me. He also told me later that they had been observing me and they knew that God's hands was upon my life; that I should just do what God had asked me to do.[5]

The unity of the Spirit was powerful among the ministers in those days and there was a single purpose to glorify Christ and impact the next generation. The ministry of one complemented and confirmed the other. It should be no wonder that God readily pronounced His blessing upon the Church in those days.

AN APOSTLE OF LOVE AND POWER

Without any doubt, Bro. Ibe was an apostle called and used of God to establish the doctrinal[6] and experiential truth about deliverance in the Body of Christ in Nigeria. Just like the Azusa parallel, the apostolic ministry of Faith Clinic, by virtue of its abundant manifestations, many of which were sensational in nature, attracted seekers as well as critics. However, Bro. Ibe continued to wage a good warfare through a commitment to love. He did not defend himself or the ministry, neither did he contend with those who found fault with him. Instead, he allowed the fruit of his ministry to speak for itself—even if the fruit was going to mature in time.

Bro. Ibe loved people to a fault. He would go to any length to save the lost. He will do anything to reconcile warring parties. He never gave up on anyone and was not easily angered. Was this one of the secrets of his power with God?

Being predisposed to loving and giving perhaps made bro. Ibe vulnerable to those who would take advantage of him. There were some, it seems, who took him for granted or abused his servant heart.[7] Notwithstanding, Bro. Ibe persisted in his love walk. He had an innocence that the devil constantly sought to corrupt. He was so tender-hearted that he could weep with anyone, anywhere. Commenting on this peculiar attribute, Aunty Pheobe had the following to say:

> Oh, Bro Ibe! He was a saint who walked this earth! He was a saint! I have not seen another like him since. Full of love! Bro. Ibe will cry unashamedly anywhere. As big as he was, he was so soft on the inside. I remember one day, during our workers' meeting. I don't know what he had heard, probably that some workers were gossiping about each other, and were fighting. I remember Bro. Ibe said to us, "Don't you know that we are all citizens of heaven? If we are, how can we be doing evil to each other?" He just burst out and started to weep. Everyone of us started to weep too! He was that tender.[8]

At least two witnesses confessed that if it were possible, Bro. Ibe would weep with the devil in order to get him converted—the same devil that wanted to destroy him![9] Did his greatest strength, therefore, become his weakness?

AN APOSTLE'S OVERSIGHT?

I have already bemoaned Faith Clinic's failure to document the great things that God was doing and teaching during the revival.[10] Bro. Ibe busied himself with pouring his life into others as a drink offering. But did he neglect the important need to pour himself unto the pages of a book? This seems to be an integral part of every apostolic commission—especially apostolic assignments that involve the establishment of precepts and doctrine. Paul wrote several letters to safeguard the gains of his apostolic ministry. The writings of William Seymour were meant to be a resource for the Pentecostal community. Did the absence of apostolic communiqués from Bro. Ibe open the door for an influx of excesses and malpractices in a ministry that began in power, simplicity and purity?[11]

Bro. Ibe also pushed himself to the limit. According to one witness, "he was a workaholic."[12] There were times when, due to much tiredness, he dozed off while driving on the expressway. Thank God for the ministry of angels!

Almost to the very last days of his life, he did not stop practising medicine. This meant that from Monday through Friday he was involved in public health service (first in UCH, then in Adeoyo Hospital and later in Ogbomosho). He did not approach his medical practice any less than the work of the ministry. To him, both vocations were service unto the Lord that involved ministering to people.

Oh, Bro. Ibe loved God so much! I have not seen another as selfless as he was.

While serving as a doctor in Adeoyo, he was transferred to Ogbomosho because of the envy of other doctors. At the O & G department where he worked, most patients always preferred to see him over any other doctor. Bro. Ibe will go to Ogbomosho in the morning and come back in the evening. As he gets back, there will be patients waiting for him in his boys quarters.

He was always spending himself. I can't call him anything less than a saint. All I know about him is beautiful.[13]

As a father of four children, Bro. Ibe had to give himself to his wife and four children too. But how much time did he have left for domestic engagements? Thank God for his rock-solid wife, Sis. Ego, who was able to take care of the home front while he served God and people. Did this continuous giving of self take its toll on Bro. Ibe? Should he have consolidated his strength and gone "full-time" with the ministry of Faith Clinic?

"I DIED LAST NIGHT!"

Bro. Ibe went to be with the Lord on the 3rd of May, 1993 at the age of 47. The manner of his departure from this world, underscores his rank before God; that he was a general indeed.

Nearly two years before this sad event, however, Bro. Ibe had a striking experience that somewhat set the course of the remaining months he was on the earth. He had fallen ill unexpectedly, and was admitted in a private ward at UCH. Bro. Okarter went to visit him one morning and just as he stepped into the ward, Bro. Ibe said, "Bro. Okarter, do you know that I died last night?"

Quite shocked at the assertion, Bro. Okarter replied, "But you are not dead."

"Yes, but I died last night," Bro. Ibe repeated, and went on to narrate an overnight experience.[14]

According to Bro. Ibe's narrative, when he died, he found himself on a long queue. People who had died from all around the world were on this queue. In front of the long line of people was an entrance, and in front of the entrance was a very huge and fierce-looking angel with a sword in his hand. Before this mighty angel was a table upon which was a massive book. The people on the queue were moving towards the angel as if they were on a conveyor belt. As each person got to the front, the heavenly being would place the tip of the sword on the book, and the book will open to a page that contained the person's records. Afterwards, only one of two words would come out of the angel's mouth: "proceed" or "depart."

Whenever the angel said "depart," a terrific wind would carry the person and take him or her into hell that had opened up its mouth to receive such a one. Each time hell opened up, Bro. Ibe heard the screams of tortured souls.

When it got to Bro. Ibe's turn, the angel placed the sword on the big book, and the page that had his records flicked open. As the angel browsed the records, he started to nod his head. When he got to the section titled LOVE, the angel paused, looked at Bro. Ibe, smiled and said, "You really loved people."

The angel went on to say to Bro. Ibe: "See, your records are splendid. In all that is written here, you did wonderfully well. But you failed in only one thing, and for this reason I will not allow you to proceed."

"You have taken the gospel around Nigeria — to every nook and corner," the angel continued. "You have preached outside Nigeria too. But you have not preached in your father's house. For this error of omission, I will send you back into the world so you can make amends. Go to your father's house and preach to them. Afterwards you can come back home."[15]

(Aunty Pheobe, in her version of the same event, had heard that Bro. Ibe was sent back to earth for more than one issue, another being his failure to keep records. Subsequent events will show that he attempted to correct both lapses).[16]

After narrating this encounter, Bro. Ibe said to Bro. Okarter, "I am healed! Jesus healed me last night! Any moment from now, the doctor will come to discharge me. Get ready, we are going to Oba for a crusade in December!"

It happened just as Bro. Ibe said it would: the doctor came and promptly discharged him.

CRUSADE IN OBA

In response to the revelation that Bro. Ibe had at the hospital, plans were made to hold an outreach in Bro.

Ibe's village; in his father's compound. He met with his father, his mother and all his siblings. He collected the addresses of all his relatives and invited each one of them to attend the meeting, which was to be held on December 31st 1991.

Unknown to him, there was a serious matter going on in the family around this time. One of the relatives had killed another relative through native charms, and he had just been excommunicated from the community. For this reason, the grieving relatives said that they would not attend the meeting if the convicted relative was invited.

Being a family of traditionalists, rivals often used charms against one another. Now that one had recently died, the bitterness was deep-seated. This, perhaps, was the situation that God wanted to heal by sending his servant with a message of peace. Bro. Ibe prayed tirelessly for the meeting, that God would intervene and glorify Himself in the midst of his family members.

Before the meeting could hold, Bro. Ibe spent hours consulting with the family members. Even on the day of the meeting, before it started, there was a large family gathering to discuss the matter. Graciously, the Lord took full control and everyone agreed to attend the programme. It was an all-night programme, patterned after the Faith Clinic Ibadan meetings.

Somehow, the word had gone round that Dr. Ibeneme was in his village. So, many people came from surrounding towns for the all-night meeting. People came from Ojonto, Nnewi, Ndemiri, Okah, Onitsha and other regions. It ended up being an open-air crusade!

God did so much that night! There were healings, deliverances, testimonies, and most of all, the salvation of many souls. All the while, Bro. Ibe's father, who was a traditionalist to the core, never believed in or supported the son's ministry. (He was meant to be the king of the land with Bro. Ibe, his first son, next-in-line to the throne. But Bro. Ibe had stopped him and refused to take any part in the position. For this reason, the crown had gone to another family). But that night, after staying awake throughout the programme, he made a confession, and said, "I have been hearing; I have been told; but today, I have seen with my eyes."[17] So, with this glorious meeting, Bro. Ibe ushered in the New Year (1992) in style, fully obeying the angel's instruction and making progress in correcting his records in the books of God.

THE LAST RECORDS?

After the successful "outside ministration" in his father's house, Bro. Ibe continued his busy schedule of practising medicine during the week and preaching the gospel all weekend (with a number of counselling or mentoring sessions wedged in-between). At some point through the year, he suffered a recurrence of the condition for which he was previously admitted in hospital. This time the condition lingered. Recall that one of the reasons why the angel had sent him back was the failure to keep some sort of records. Was this the reason why there was relapse in his health? We can only speculate. However, there were reports that Bro. Ibe probably tried to do something about this in the final days of his life.[18]

From the point of relapse in 1992, Bro. Ibe's conditioned persisted; and in spite of a drop in his level of strength, he continued working in the hospital and ministering for the Lord. Some were not even aware that he was sick during this time. It was after he went for treatment in London that he experienced a sharp deterioration in his health.

The entire Body of Christ was concerned when the news about Bro. Ibe's illness came to light. Many prayer sessions were held on his behalf. The news got as far as London, where Colin Dye did not only announce the incident, but also organised fasting and prayer sessions on his behalf.[19]

During the last Faith Clinic programme that Bro. Ibe attended, he was scheduled to take the second message, the exhortation leading to the deliverance ministrations. When the time came for him to come up stage, he did not show up. He was eventually found in the office, dictating some important things to the secretary at the time. He told those who had come for him he would soon come out. Eventually, he asked someone to take the session for him. At that moment, the things he was dictating were more important than the deliverance session. The general dictated well into the night.[20] Evidently, he was getting ready to return back to his heavenly home.

"THE VEHICLE HAS ARRIVED!"

As painful as Bro. Ibe's death was, there is so much affirmation about where his final destination was. His wife, who was there with him throughout his life and also at the point of death, said confidently that "Ibe saw the Lord; I know he made heaven."[21]

Several people were in the house on the day that God's general departed. It seemed they were all summoned specially to witness this homecoming. For instance, Remi Tejumola had not been at Faith Clinic for months before this day, but had a longing that morning to see Bro. Ibe. When he came into House 5, Bro. Ibe asked him, "How did you know to come?"[22]

Bro. Okarter, who was the prayer band leader at the time, had organised teams of people to hold prayer vigils at Bro. Ibe's home everyday. His turn was on Sunday. The day after the vigil, he went to his office, only for the Holy Spirit to prompt him strongly to go to Bro. Ibe's residence. When the promptings did not subside, he obeyed and was able to witness the momentous occasion.[23]

My mother, too, who had since reduced her attendance at Faith Clinic since becoming the Personal Assistant of Rev. Victor Adeyemi in 1991, received an unexpected and unusual message from Aunty Pheobe. She was told Bro. Ibe was asking for her. On hearing this message, she took off and went to visit him. It was a timely, Monday morning visit.[24] Some other people who were at the house include, Mr. & Mrs. Banks Ejina, Rev. Kuti, Rev. David Adeleke, Funmi Fawoye, and his wife, Sis. Ego.[25]

Esther Olulaja, my mother, recalls a series of events that happened when she got to Bro. Ibe's residence:

> As I got to House 5, there were some ministers already in the house. Sis. Ego was also present. Bro. Ibe was seated on a three-sitter settee, but seemed to

be gasping for air. His cheeks would fill up with air and then he will release it by slightly opening his mouth. As I approached him, I tried to get Bro. Ibe's attention by making signs with my hand and also saying, "It is Esther, it is Esther." Acknowledging my presence, he lifted up his hand to me and I placed my hand on his. As I did this he began to recite the priestly blessing of Numbers 6:

The Lord bless you, and keep you

The Lord make His face to shine upon you

And be gracious to you

The Lord lift up His countenance upon you

And give you peace.

After this, I sat by him. He was restless. Ministers were praying for him.

Suddenly he said, "Where are the elders?... They are coming... They are seated... The elders are seated and are having a meeting..."[26]

Bro. Okarter, who had arrived before my mother, also recollects some unforgettable events that took place on that day:

The moment I opened the door and came in, Bro. Ibe gathered himself, like Elisha did in 2 Kings 13, and sat down. Then he said to me, "Okarter, do you know the battle will end today?" I said, "Yes sir."

Then he held his two ears and said, "Preach righteousness! Preach righteousness! You hear?" Again I said, "Yes sir."

"Because God is angry," he continued. "God is angry. Everyone is preaching prosperity, prosperity, and the souls of men are going to hell; nobody is talking to them. You must preach righteousness, do you hear?" I said, "Yes sir."

He then said, "There will be a great rain here today... I want to eat cake."[27]

Bro. Okarter and Remi Tejumola both went to get some cake for Bro. Ibe and he had some to eat. He also asked for a glass of water. Afterwards, he said, "The vehicle will soon arrive."

After a while, Bro. Ibe asked for his children to be brought in from school. Only the two daughters were allowed out of school because the boys were having lessons.

My mother, Esther Olulaja, remembers the moment the children came in:

> Soon afterwards, his children came in. The moment they were all inside, and without any prior warning, a whirlwind seemed to fill the room. The wind was so much that the curtains were being raised and paper blown from the table. At this, I decided to leave, not wanting the rain to keep me from going back to the office. As I got back to the car, the news came that Bro. Ibe had died. I came back into the room to see him motionless in the chair.[28]

Bro. Okarter's recollections of what happened after Bro. Ibe asked for his children are more detailed:

Bro. Ibe began to say, "Now, you elders, you have

gathered; bring the record books. God, is there anything else that I have not done? Does anybody have anything to accuse me of, let him say it now."

By that time, I was holding him like a baby; he was just unstable. Then I began to bind and loose; I was casting out demons. But he slapped my hand and said, "Stop it!" He began to say that he wanted to go, that this world was too rotten and he did not want to stay any longer. He said he had finished his work.

"God, all the places you have sent me, I have gone. Is there anything else you want me to do that I have not done? Lord I want to come home." He was begging to depart.

The elders that he was speaking with, we could not see; but they were discussing. I was still holding him when he said, "The vehicle has arrived! The vehicle has arrived! Let somebody pray!"

After I had prayed, he said, "Now, may the grace of our Lord Jesus Christ, and the love of God, and fellowship of the Holy Spirit be with us now and forevermore, A-a-a..."

As he opened his mouth to say "Amen," I placed my hand over his mouth to stop him, but he knocked my hand off. The next thing I heard was a loud exclamation, "Ye-e-e-e!" and with his mouth open, he gave up the ghost.[29]

The sun was shining brightly in the sky prior to this time, but the moment God's general left with the heavenly chariots, there was a mighty wind and heavy downpour. The rain did not last for too long. In just the way it started, the rain soon stopped and the bright skies returned. The general had gone home to be with his Lord.

Sis. Ego then called Dr. Victor Adegboye and said, "Brother, Bro. Ibe is gone." The doctor came straight-away, checked him and pronounced him dead. He was buried in his hometown, and as he specifically instructed before his death, the Faith Clinic programme in Ibadan was not cancelled on the weekend of his burial.[30]

Esther Olulaja recalls:

> I attended the burial in Anambra, which was in the form of an outreach. Bro. Ibe's body was laid in state in the house and ministrations were going on out-side. He was buried in his compound.
>
> Everyone said he was a general, and by the manner in which he left this world, he truly was.[31]

All those who knew Bro. Ibe, especially those who were involved with the ministry of Faith Clinic, were shaken by his death. The words of Mary Owoade sums up the common feeling among those who loved him:

> When Bro. Ibe died, I was devastated. Although I did not backslide, I became afraid of the ministry of deliverance. I wondered how a man so used of God could die in his prime.
>
> It was obvious, however, that he was ready to go. We prayed and prayed. When he gave up the ghost, I screamed and wept. I can never forget him.[32]

Many, as Sis. Mary said, had prayed for his recovery, but, knowing that he had finished his assignment in the world, it pleased the Lord to take him away.

This is the testimony of Scripture:

"The righteous perish, and no one ponders it in his heart; devout men are taken away, and no one understands that the righteous are taken away to be spared from evil. Those who walk uprightly enter into peace; they find rest as they lie in death."[33]

11

DO WE NEED
ANOTHER REVIVAL?

B efore we consider, by way of conclusion, the question that this chapter poses, let us attempt to answer another one that is closely related to it: *Why do revivals seem to subside after a few years?*

The Azusa Street revival that God used to restore the baptism of the Holy Spirit with the accompanying spiritual gift of tongues back to the Church, began in 1904. Not too long afterwards, from 1906, the intensity of the revival at the Azusa Street location started to wane until it finally ceased.[1] The Faith Clinic revival, which was the primary means for restoring the practical knowledge and experience of casting out devils in the name of Jesus to the Church in Nigeria, also had a beginning (1983) and an eventual ending (1993). The ministry has now fizzled into a local church situated in their permanent location at Ijokodo, Ibadan;[2] they still minister deliverance to those who come for counselling, but the crowds are no longer thronging the services. Other revivals have "suffered" a similar fate.[3] Why is this so?

One perspective is the restorative agenda that God had in mind for some of these revivals. It seems that God usually has specific purposes that He seeks to accomplish with some of these moves, and once these purposes are fulfilled, things begin to wind down. For Azusa, it was the restoration of Pentecost and the gift of tongues; for Faith Clinic, it was the restoration of deliverance. The length of the revivals is not as important as what God sought to achieve through them.

Another consideration is the fact that God is more interested in spreading the knowledge of His glory abroad than just concentrating it in one spot. His vision is for the glory to permeate everywhere as the waters cover the sea.[4] It is not possible to contain the glory of God in a single place. Even people will change their locations from time to time as the purposes of their lives unfold.

The moment Jesus died on the cross, the veil that held the shekinah glory of God in the physical holy of holies was rent from top to bottom, signifying a new era where man could access God's presence from anywhere, and His presence could abide with man everywhere.[5] The purpose of a particular location in revival, therefore, be it a temple in Jerusalem, 312 Azusa Street or House 5 in UCH, is to trigger an unending spread so that God's glory fills all in all.

Not knowing this, people are always tempted to conserve the glory in a place or region. When Nimrod, in pre-Abrahamic times, tried to confine mankind to a particular geographical location, God confused the people's language and scattered them to the ends of the earth.[6] When the Church in Jerusalem overlooked the go-ye-into-all-the-world commission of Christ, God scattered the disciples from Jerusalem to the surrounding regions of Judea and Samaria.[7] It is an historical fact that a generation is likely to settle with past success and neglect the need to break further ground. This tendency is what causes revival movements to become monuments after a season.

One more reason is the fact that whenever God does something new, or restores something that had once been, He usually does it in an unmistakeable and attention-grabbing way. The exodus of Israel from Egypt to Canaan was a spectacular process that included spectacular events like the slaying of Egypt's firstborn children and the parting of the Red Sea. The news of these feats went abroad and struck fear in the hearts of surrounding peoples.[8] The coming of the Holy Spirit on the day of Pentecost for the inauguration of the Church happened in a most peculiar way.[9] The restoration of Pentecost at the turn of the 20th Century was with powerful waves of unusual occurrences. Similarly, the restoration of the believers authority to cast out devils through Faith Clinic came with unusual grace for spectacular miracles.

However, after the "announcement" and establishment of what God had in mind, the waves subside so that the substance that the waves came to deliver could abide in the earth. In other words, after the dramatic revival at Azusa, the substance of the Spirit and His gifts have remained with us. After the powerful revival at Faith Clinic, the knowledge of how to cast out devils is now with us. Tidal waves do not stay above sea levels for ever;

they soon come down. Surfers ride on the waves; ships sail on the seas. It is still the same substance; same force, and same power. The One who reveals Himself in the wind, fire and earthquake is the same One who reveals Himself in the still small voice. There is no difference.

In other words, the blessing of Azusa is meant to function in us today. The essence of Faith Clinic should be the experience of every believer. The same power that raised Christ from the dead dwells in those who believe to this day! So, irrespective of the circumstances that contribute to the "winding down" of a revival in a particular location,[10] its abiding benefits are of greater significance.

ANOTHER REVIVAL?

So, do we need another revival? Well, if the revival quest is for the purpose of restoring what had already been restored, then we do not need another (unless we are experiencing another spiritual "dark age"). We do not need another Azusa because we understand the truth about the baptism of the Spirit today. We do not need another Faith Clinic era if it is for the purpose of establishing the truth about our authority to cast out devils. God has used Bro. Ibe to accomplish this. If all we long for is the euphoria of the past — the excitement of the 1900s or the thrills of the 1980s — then we do not need another awakening. We cannot recreate Azusa experiences or Faith Clinic meetings just for the sake of them.

However, we need a move of God if the gains of past revivals are no longer abounding. We need a revival if the spiritual labours of yesterday are not producing fruit today. We need a revival when a people forget the standards set by their forefathers and carelessly shift ancient landmarks. We need a heaven-rending and an earth-shaking revival when the articles of gold and silver in God's temple are substituted with inferior articles of iron and bronze. We need a spiritual awakening when the wells of past revivals no longer spring forth with the life that once sustained and blessed the early beneficiaries. Oh yes, we need a revival when the presence of God is no longer permeating our earthly space!

The Faith Clinic revival happened just over twenty years ago. Bro. Ibe went to be with the Lord not too long ago. God's purpose for the Faith Clinic revival; the reason why He raised a General in Bro. Ibe, was for believers to understand their authority in Christ and become terrors to the camp of the enemy. Sadly, many believers are today running away from the enemy in fear of their lives! They are ignorant of the mighty power that is at work in them.

A few times, during the life of Bro. Ibe, people will see him on the street and the demons in them will start manifesting: "We went to Port Harcourt, you drove us out! We have come to Ibadan and you are following us about! Why are you terrorising us?"[11] Is this not what the devils said about Christ and Paul?[12] What are they saying about us today?

THE FRUIT OF REVIVAL

There is another cogent reason why we need to seek God for a move of His Spirit amongst us once again, and that is for a harvest of souls and the raising of true disciples.

During a move of God, Holy Spirit-convictions are deep and conversions are real. These are non-negotiable criteria for producing disciples that are sold out for God.

The Faith Clinic revival produced a generation of firebrand ministers. Many young men and women who came in contact with the reality of God, developed a hunger for Him and a desire to be used by Him. Today, many are standing firm in the Lord and manifesting the glory of God. Such is the fruit of any sustained move of God. However, the price paid for their emergence was high.

THE PRICE OF REVIVAL

There can be no revival today if we are not ready to pay the price of total submission to God and death to self. Those who God will use as vessels of revival cannot do their own bidding or seek their own glory. Bro. Ibe was totally in love with God and had no personal agenda of his own. He was selfless to a fault. Besides, the ministry required him to give his all—and he did. Those who followed him learnt to do the same.

Whenever any deliverance case was "difficult" and prolonged, Bro. Ibe and the Faith Clinic team never gave up. There were always some who would stay with the case until the very end. Even when they were evidently exhausted physically, they will keep on with the deliverance until the last demon leaves. They were that committed.

The price of prayer in any revival can never be overemphasised. Bro. Ibe was given to much prayer, and the

prayer culture was passed on to all the Faith Clinic ministers. There is no other way to be full of God and His glory
without a commitment to prayer.

Finally, in the words of Sis. Ego, Bro. Ibe "had the
heart of a child. He could weep with anybody." This was
a display of total selflessness; the abandonment of self.
She added that Bro. Ibe gave up everything for the call,
including his privacy. How many are ready to pay such a
price today? God gave him grace to stand in his calling; it
was not something he assumed upon himself.[13]

A PEOPLE ON THE GO!

The will of God for sending revival is for every believer
to become carriers of His glory; we are all meant to be
revivalists in our fields of endeavour. We are all deliver-
ers of people and nations. The life of Bro. Ibe and the
revival at Faith Clinic has shown us just a glimpse of
what this could mean in a lifetime.

That God sent us this revival in Nigeria, through the
instrumentality of Nigerian believers, is not accidental. It
has played a part in fulfilling the prophecy over the
nation that God would use Nigerians around the world
to spread the gospel. The Faith Clinic revival raised a
workforce for the Kingdom of God; many who have gone
to the ends of the earth with the message of salvation and
deliverance. There is, however, a need for today's generation of ministers to build upon yesterday's momentum
and raise the next generation of Kingdom workers. If our
hands are slack in this task or the next generation are not
responding as they should, then we most definitely need

a revival from God. Without another mighty move of God in our land, we may not fully fulfil our prophetic destiny as a nation.

God's desire is for the fruit of every past revival to accompany us everywhere we go. We have no excuse for living below the standards of His Word and experiencing less than the fathers of faith experienced in the past. Inspired by their stories and grateful for their legacy, may we now take the baton, do the will of the Master and finish the work committed to us:

> Go ye into all the world, and preach the gospel to every creature... And these signs shall follow them that believe; In my name shall they cast out devils (the fruit of the *Faith Clinic revival*); they shall speak with new tongues (the fruit of the *Azusa Street revival*)... And they went forth, and preached everywhere, the Lord working with them, and confirming the word with signs following. Amen.[14]

This is our heritage. This is our commission. This is *now* our prayer:

> O Lord, revive thy work in the midst of the years, in the midst of the years make known; in wrath remember mercy.[15]

> God, I've heard what our ancestors say about you, and I'm stopped in my tracks, down on my knees. Do among us what you did among them. Work among us as you worked among them. And as you bring judgement, as you surely must, remember mercy.[16]

DO YOU HAVE A "FAITH CLINIC" STORY TO TELL?

Were you an eye-witness of the glory and power of God at Faith Clinic in the 1980s and 1990s?

Did you get saved, healed, delivered or filled with the Holy Spirit at Faith Clinic?

Did you attend the Faith Clinic Bible School?

Were you one of the Faith Clinic ministers?

Did you have the privilege of meeting or relating with Bro. Ibe?

Are you in possession of any of his books, audio or video recordings?

We would like to hear from you!

Please send your story to:

tokunboemmanuel@yahoo.co.uk

OR

www.facebook.com/TheFaithClinicRevival

Thanks and God bless!

NOTES

AUTHOR'S PREFACE

1. The day after my conversion in August 1986, I supernaturally received the gift and grace to write. For nineteen hours, I wrote mysteries and prophecies about the end-times without any pre-meditation. The exercise book that I wrote in that day was given to Dr. Ibeneme and it has remained in his custody to this day.

2. I attended Faith Clinic regularly during holidays (as a student in the Obafemi Awolowo University, Ile-Ife) but did not join the ministry team due to distance and my constant absence. Notwithstanding, I was part of a fellowship started by my late father in our local church at the time (New Salem Church, Felele). My father was a dedicated minister at Faith Clinic. So, barely six months into my new life in Christ, the grace to cast out devils rubbed off on me mightily.

ACKNOWLEDGEMENTS

1. I edited some of the quoted material slightly for grammatical adjustments without changing their original essence. *Sade's Testimony* I have reproduced without any alteration whatsoever.

FOREWORD

1. 1 Corinthians 2:14

2. Ephesians 6:12

3. Luke 10:18

4. Colossians 2:15

INTRODUCTION

1. www.cleartheology.com/topic/Revival/Revival%2005.pdf

2. This is an authentic statement even though many who claim to be "deliverance ministers" or "deliverance ministries" today are not

exhibiting the simplicity, purity and transparency that was present in the life of Dr. Ibeneme and the operations of Faith Clinic.

3.   A humble admission of one of the ministers, Christopher Okarter, during an interview. Although, a video documentation was purportedly done, entitled *A Day in Faith Clinic* (discussion with Remi Tejumola). I am still searching for a copy of this and other recordings.

4.   Incidentally, I learnt towards the end of this project (from Remi Tejumola and Adolphus Iteghie), contrary to my prior understanding, that Bro. Ibe did write a few books, including: *The Cross, Who Are You?*, *Dynamite Your Faith Into Action* and in later years, *Deliverance Lecture Notes*. Up until the time of going to press, I could not lay my hands on copies of any of these titles. The books, according to Remi Tejumola, did not become popular, because he had written on topics "outside" his main area of specialty (although, it is not clear whether they were written before Faith Clinic began). Add to this, a below-average reading culture and appreciation for books in Nigeria — a situation that still persists to this day.

5.   Frank Bartleman (1871-1936) was "an author, evangelist and missionary." He was "a prolific writer" and "the most significant social commentator of early Pentecostalism... Bartleman is best remembered for his chronicles of the 1906 Pentecostal revival at Los Angeles, including events leading up to and immediately following the revival." He published a collection of his articles about the revival in a book titled, *How Pentecost Came to Los Angeles*. (Source www.frankbartleman.blogspot.com).

6.   The book *Fire on the Earth*, a collection of all the editions of this publication and commissioned for the Azusa Street Centurial celebrations, has the following in its introduction: "Between September 1906 and May 1908 William J. Seymour and the leadership of the revival published thirteen editions of this paper that they called *The Apostolic Faith*. The name expressed their belief that through this revival, the apostolic faith of the New Testament was being restored to the churches." (Hyatt Eddie, *Fire on the Earth*, Creation House 2006).

7.   www.azusastreet.org/williamjseymour.htm

8. Ibid.

9. For instance, pictures were taken in a pre-digital era; and almost all the films have either been lost or damaged due to poor storage and the forces of nature (interview with Adolphus Iteghie, Christopher Okarter and others).

10. Ojo, Matthews. *The End-Time Army: Charismatic Movements in Modern Nigeria* (Trenton: Africa World Press, 2006).

11. Abodunde, Ayodeji. *A Heritage of Faith: A History of Christianity in Nigeria* (Ibadan: PriceWater House 2009).

12. Mr. Abodunde, author of *A Heritage of Faith*, told me that having learnt about the happenings at Faith Clinic, he visited the Faith Clinic office to ask for any form of documentation — writings or audio-visual recordings — that he could use for his work but none could be provided. The visit and request were confirmed by Adolphus Iteghie, the current National Director of Faith Clinic.

13. Readers are invited to send their experiences and stories for future editions and publications.

14. http://www.blogspot.faithclinicibadan.com

15. https://www.facebook.com/groups/faithclinic/?fref=ts

16. Psalm 102:18

CHAPTER 1:
A WOMB FOR REVIVAL

1. Abodunde, Ayodeji. *A Heritage of Faith: A History of Christianity in Nigeria* (Ibadan: PriceWater House 2009).

2. Ibid.

3. Interview with Rev. Emiko Amotsuka.

4. Ibid.

5. From a message by Evangelist Matthew Owojaiye, delivered at Faith Clinic's Prophetic Prayer Conference in May 2011.

6. Bill Isaacs-Sodeye, *From Medicine to Miracles* (http://www.healingloveofchrist.org/billslifestory/book.htm).

7. Ibid.

8. Correspondence with Professor Bill Isaacs-Sodeye.

9. Interview with Adolphus Iteghie

10. Abodunde, Ayodeji. *A Heritage of Faith: A History of Christianity in Nigeria* (Ibadan: PriceWater House 2009).

11. http://www.elifeonline.net/elife17-Aug-Sept/interview-madubuko.htm

12. This counsel is perfectly correct. The sacrifice of Christ delivers man totally from the kingdom of darkness and translates him into the Kingdom of light. In experiential and practical terms, both from Scripture and church history, it is sometimes imperative for past demonic influences and strongholds to be broken through prayer before a new believer can enjoy his or her newly-found freedom in Christ, especially when there's been involvement with the occult or other ritualistic covenants. Upon encountering Christ, Mary Magdalene had seven demons cast of her (Luke 8:1,2); many who heeded the message of Philip in Samaria, who were previously under demonic influences, also demons cast out of them. The result "was great joy in that city" (Acts 8:5-8).

13. Lifeway Magazine, September-October 2008 edition.

14. http://www.elifeonline.net/elife17-Aug-Sept/interview-madubuko.htm; confirmed during discussion with Adolphus Iteghie.

CHAPTER 2:
THE BIRTH OF A MOVEMENT

1. As a specialist in gynaecology, Bro. Ibe worked at UCH, Adeoyo Hospital and in Ogbomosho.

2. Rev. Victor Amosun's response to a questionnaire.

3. Interview with Pastor Chris Asudemade.

4. Interview with Sis. Gbemi Olaleye.

5. Mark 1:41, for example.

6. Mark 7:31-37, for example.

7. Luke 11:14.

8. Interview granted by Rev. Dr. (Mrs.) Ego Ibeneme to Tribune Newspaper (http://tribune.com.ng/sat/index.php/women-affairs/7623-if-youre-not-married-quite-a-percentage-of-respect-

is-removed-from-you.html).

9. Interview with Christopher Okarter.

10. See Acts 11:26

11. Interview with Pastor Remi Tejumola.

CHAPTER 3:
FROM HOUSE 5 TO THE LECTURE THEATRE

1. Luke 4:36,37.

2. See Luke 11:24-26

3. Interview with Pastor Remi Tejumola.

4. http://www.wikisozo.com

5. This probably refers to Bro. Ibe's involvement with I.V.C.U. or another fellowship that met at the Chapel of Resurrection, UI, as Faith Clinic never used the Chapel for meetings, and had not started by the year 1981.

6. http://wikisozo.com/story/read/25841/deaconess-abigails-salvation-story

7. http://wikisozo.com/story/read/14833/from-darkness-to-lightblw-oau

8. Interview with Pastor Oluwole.

9. Lekan Oyegoke, *Research in African Literatures* (Bloomington IN: Indiana University Press 1998?), pp 133-137.

10. Ibid.

11. The new name for Adamasingba Stadium.

12. Lekan Oyegoke, *Research in African Literatures* (Bloomington IN: Indiana University Press 1998?), pp 133-137.

13. Revelation 12:11.

CHAPTER 4:

MANIFESTATIONS OF POWER!

1. http://tejumolapneuma.blogspot.com/2009/08/holy-spirit-moves-3.html

2. John 4:48

3. Mark 5:25,26

4. Matthew 11:28

5. A full explanation and analysis of Bro. Ibe's insight into deliverance and the things he taught from Scripture about the operations of the devil (demonology) are more appropriate for another book.

6. Interview with Christopher Okarter.

7. http://tejumolapneuma.blogspot.com/2009/09/believers-authority-my-adventures-1.html

8. Interview with Christopher Okarter.

9. Christie Ifebueme, *Alive at Last!* (Ibadan: Joy of Salvation Deliverance Ministry, 2004).

10. Ibid.

11. Ibid.

12. Ibid.

13. Ibid.

14. Ibid.

15. http://tejumolapneuma.blogspot.com/2009/08/holy-spirit-moves-2.html

CHAPTER 5:

LABOURERS FOR THE HARVEST

1. Matthew 9:37

2. Matthew 9:38

3. Interview with Rev. Funke Adetuberu

4. Ibid.

5. Ibid.

6. Interview with Bishop Marcus Benson

7. Ibid.

8. Ibid.

9. Rev. Victor Amosun's response to a questionnaire.

10.   Some of the ones found include the following:

Prophetess Stella Sam-Ekhator of *Destiny Women International* (USA): "I know that it is no coincidence that while I was still ministering in Africa, I was trained by one of the best in the field of deliverance then, *Late Dr. Ibeneme*. It was truly awesome to see the change in people's countenance and lives after being set free from demonic oppression.

(http://destinywomen.org/deliverance.html)

Bishop Marcus Benson's profile, *Global Faith Dimensions* (Ireland): "His ministry career began with *the Faith Clinic Inc.*, Ibadan, Oyo State, Nigeria"

(http://globalfaithdimensions.org/marcus-benson.html)

Apostle Stephanie Olu Ojo's profile, *Voice of Victory International Church* (Ireland): "Apostle Stephanie Olu Ojo... is called uniquely by the Lord as an Apostle, Teacher and Pastor. She accepted Christ at an early age and was mentored by Archbishop Benson Idahosa of the Church of God Mission and *Dr. I.K.U. Ibeneme, the founder of the Faith Clinic where she attended the Bible School of the Faith Clinic Inc,* a deliverance ministry based in Ibadan, Nigeria.

(http://www.voiceofvictoryinternationalchurch.org/contact-us.php).

Other references found but whose links were no longer active at the time of writing include: www.jesuspoweroutreach.org (by **Evangelist Oguazi Onyemobi**); and www.possibilityassembly.org.uk (by **Pastor Lanre Jegede**).

11.   http://tejumolapneuma.blogspot.com/2009/08/holy-spirit-moves.html (He also recounts this experience in his book, *The Holy Ghost Invasion*, pp 29-30).

12.   http://tejumolapneuma.blogspot.com/2009/08/holy-spirit-moves.html

13.   Remi Tejumola, *The Holy Ghost Invasion* (Ibadan: New Life Global Outreach Ministries, 2003), pp 32.

14.   http://tejumolapneuma.blogspot.com/2010/04/soldier-gone-to-headquater.html

15.   Interview with Aunty Pheobe Olulode.

16. She now bears the name Olulaja.

17. Interview with Pastor (Mrs.) Esther Olulaja.

18. Interview with Bro. Kunle Oladiran.

19. Interview with Pastor Mike Ayodele.

20. 1 Corinthians 11:1.

21. Interview with Pastor Mike Ayodele.

22. Now Mary Owoade.

23. Interview with Sis. Mary Owoade.

24. Ibid.

25. Ibid.

26. Interview with Christopher Okarter.

27. Remi Tejumola, *The Holy Ghost Invasion* (Ibadan: New Life Global Outreach Ministries, 2003), pp 56.

CHAPTER 6:

WORD EXPLOSION AT THE STADIUM!

1. See Timothy's testimony on page

2. Interview with Aunty Pheobe Olulode.

3. Greg Alabi's response to a questionnaire.

4. Rev. Victor Amosun's response to a questionnaire.

5. Ibid.

6. Interview with Segun Akintola.

7. Formerly Temitope Olawuyi.

8. Interview with Pastor Mike Ayodele.

9. Patrick Anwuzia, for instance, attended the school but did not complete the course. He went on to start Zoe Ministries where he ministered "deliverance" to people. The simplicity, purity and sincerity that were marks of Faith Clinic were absent from Zoe Ministries. Besides, the deliverance process was commercialised and before long, the ministry was brought into disrepute. He went through Faith Clinic Bible School but the school did not go through him. (From an interview with Rev. Victor Amosun and

other Faith Clinic ministers).

10. Rev. Victor Amosun's response to a questionnaire.

CHAPTER 7
SCEPTICISM, CRITICISM AND OPPOSITION

1. Acts 2:12,13

2. www.en.wikipedia.org/wiki/Azusa_Street

3. Matthew 12:23,24

4. As noted earlier, discussions on the theology of deliverance is more appropriate in a separate treatise. Although I have lamented the inadequate amount of documentation of Bro. Ibe's teachings, it is reported that he intended to produce a four-part manual of his insights. Unfortunately, only the first was published, a pamphlet he titled, *Deliverance Lecture Notes*. I have not yet laid my hands on a copy of this pamphlet too. The search is still on!

5. Christopher Okarter, Jonah Mbadugha and Adolphus Iteghie were all members AOG in Mokola. They shared that they were severely persecuted and eventually ex-communicated for getting involved with Faith Clinic.

6. Interview with Jonah Mbadugha.

7. Rev. Victor Amosun's answer's to a questionnaire.

8. Interview with Aunty Pheobe Olulode.

9. Interview with Mary Owoade.

10. Interview with Christopher Okarter.

11. See John 20:25-29.

CHAPTER 8:
OUTSIDE MINISTRATIONS

1. Correspondence with Pastor Alex Adegboye.

2. Interview with Pastor Alex Adegboye.

3. Scripture Union.

4. Fellowship of Christian Students.

5. Society of Christian Movements.

6. Christian Students Social Movement.

7. Interview with Pastor Alex Adegboye.

8. Correspondence with Pastor Alex Adegboye.

9. Interview with Pastor Alex Adegboye.

10. Interview with Aunty Christie Ifebueme.

11. Interview with Bishop Marcus Benson.

12. Testimony of Aunty Christie during Faith Clinic's Prophetic Prayer Conference, 2010. She repeated the same testimony during an interview with her in 2011.

13. Testimony of Aunty Christie during Faith Clinic's Prophetic Prayer Conference, 2010.

14. Rev. Victor Amosun's response to a questionnaire.

15. Interview with Christopher Okarter.

16. Philippians 4:1,2.

17. Interview with Christopher Okarter.

18. http://tejumolapneuma.blogspot.com/2009/08/holy-spirit-moves-4_16.html

19. Remi Tejumola, *The Holy Ghost Invasion* (Ibadan: New Life Global Outreach Ministries, 2003), pp 29-30.

20. Interview with Christopher Okarter.

21. Ibid.

22. This was Christopher Okarter, who also related the story.

23. Interview with Christopher Okarter.

24. Ibid.

25. Isaiah 49:24,25.

CHAPTER 9:

OVERFLOWING GLORY!

1. Interview with Remi Tejumola.

2. Ibid.

3. The Faith Clinic leadership eventually developed the idea of a local church, which is now situated on their permanent ground at Ijokodo, Ibadan. This, however, was not a part of the original operation.

4. Now Dr. Ope Akinnusi.

5. Interview with Dr. Ope Akinnusi.

6. Now Olabisi Onabanjo University.

7. Interview with Rev. Alric Amona.

8. Correspondence with Pastor Lanre Jegede.

9. Now Salem Gospel Mission.

10. These were the meetings where I began to minister deliverance, barely six months after giving my life to Christ! I travelled to Ibadan almost every week from Ile-Ife throughout my first year on campus.

11. Interview with Christopher Okarter.

12. Now Mary Ajayi.

13. Interview with Pastor Mary Ajayi.

14. Interview with Bishop Marcus Benson.

15. Ibid.

16. Interview with Pastor Timothy Babatunde.

17. Ibid.

18. Ibid.

19. Interview with Christopher Okarter.

20. Phone interview with Pastor Chucks Amaefule.

21. en.wikipedia.org/wiki/Pan_Am_Flight_103

22. John 20:30,31; 21:25 (John's comment "that even the world itself could not contain the books that should be written" is perhaps a simile, but putting into consideration the way scrolls were hand-written in those days, he could well be making a statement of fact).

CHAPTER 10:

A GENERAL'S EXIT

1. Roberts Liardon popularised the term "God's generals" through his series of books (the *God's Generals* series) that chronicle the life and ministry of people used by God over the years.

2. Interview with Bishop Marcus Benson.

3. Interview with Pastor Alex Adegboye.

4. Interview with Chris Asudemade.

5. Akinwale Johnson, *Excelling in Your Ministry* (unpublished manuscript).

6. Bro. Ibe taught extensively on demonology and deliverance, but, as noted earlier, a detailed discussion of his insights are more suitable in a separate volume.

7. Rev. Victor Amosun's response to a questionnaire.

8. Interview with Aunty Pheobe Olulode.

9. Interview with Sis. Ego Ibeneme. Also, testimony of Chris Asudemade about a statement made by Pastor Olubi Johnson.

10. See Introduction, pg

11. First, as the crowd grew at Faith Clinic over the years, so did the number of people needing deliverance and the number of ministers that joined the team. Very subtly, some began to substitute the pure manifestation of the Spirit's power with methodology and formulae. Second, it was inevitable that some would give undue focus on the sensational aspect of deliverance, especially those conducted outside the context of Faith Clinic. Lastly, now that the concept of deliverance was becoming known and accepted, there were some who began to operate in this ministry without the heart of God and heart for the people that was evident in Bro. Ibe and the Faith Clinic team. Some began to merchandise the deliverance process. Unfortunately, some of these people caught the idea of engaging in deliverance by observing what was happening in Faith Clinic.

12. Interview with Pastor (Mrs.) Esther Olulaja.

13. Interview with Aunty Pheobe Olulode.

14. Interview with Christopher Okarter.

15. Ibid.

16. Interview with Aunty Pheobe Olulode.

17. Interview with Christopher Okarter.

18. The booklet, Deliverance Lecture Notes, were released around this time. Bro. Ibe had intended to produce a series of four booklets, but only one was finished before his departure to glory.

19. Interview with Aunty Pheobe Olulode. The Lord had told her that her work with Faith Clinic had come to an end and that she would spend six months in the United Kingdom before returning to Nigeria. After handing over the Bible School files, she travelled to London. It was while attending KT that she heard the announcement of Bro. Ibe's illness. She was devastated because she had no previous idea that anything was wrong with him.

20. Interview with Christopher Okarter. I am yet to find a recording of that night's dictations or a transcript of what was dictated.

21. Interview with Sis. Ego Ibeneme, as well as public statements during the Faith Clinic Prophetic Prayer Conferences.

22. Discussion with Remi Tejumola.

23. Interview with Christopher Okarter.

24. Interview with Pastor (Mrs.) Esther Olulaja.

25. Interview with Christopher Okarter.

26. Interview with Pastor (Mrs.) Esther Olulaja.

27. Interview with Christopher Okarter.

28. Interview with Pastor (Mrs.) Esther Olulaja.

29. Interview with Christopher Okarter.

30. Ibid.

31. Interview with Pastor (Mrs.) Esther Olulaja.

32. Interview with Mary Owoade.

33. Isaiah 57:1-2 NIV

CHAPTER 11:
DO WE NEED ANOTHER REVIVAL?

1. Different accounts state different end dates. The common ones are 1906 and 1914.

2. The Chapel of Faith is situated along Sango-Eleyele Road, Ijokodo/WAEC Junction, Ibadan.

3. For example, the Welsh Revival (1904-1905); or the American Healing revival (1940s-1950s).

4. Numbers 14:21; Psalm 72:19; Isaiah 11:9; Habakkuk 2:14.

5. Mark 15:37,38.

6. Genesis 11:1-9.

7. Acts 8:1,4.

8. Joshua 2:9-11.

9. Acts 2:1-12.

10. Many reasons can easily be given for the slow-down of a revival in a particular location. The death of Stephen contributed to the scattering of the church in Jerusalem; two ladies, reacting to William Seymour's marriage to Jeanne Evans Moore in 1908, left with the main Azusa Street mission mailing list, crippling *The Apostolic Faith Newspaper*; some "witchcraft" operations halted the ministry of Evans Roberts and thus the Welsh revival; certainly the death of Bro. Ibe was the final incident that signified the decline of the revival at Faith Clinic.

11. Interview with Christopher Okarter.

12. Interview with Sis. Ego Ibeneme.

13. See Mark 1:23,24; Acts 19:15.

14. Mark 16:17,20 (author's application in italics).

15. Habakkuk 3:2.

16. Habakkuk 3:2 (The Message translation).

OTHER BOOKS BY TOKUNBO EMMANUEL

1. Sharing the Word of God
2. Rediscovering God
3. Revival in the Desert
4. 31 Nuggets of Inspiration
5. The Glory of Young Men
6. The Charismatic Agenda
7. Ultimate Destiny
8. Selah Verses
9. Run, Church Run!
10. The Secret of Abraham
11. The Greatest Well-digger in the World
12. A Scribe's Inspiration
13. The Shift of a Lifetime
14. The Mandate of Paul
15. The Wells of Isaac
16. The Destiny of Jacob

THE BWAM MANDATE

Publish culturally-relevant, life-transforming
Kingdom books and resources.

Distribute strategically and promote widely
Kingdom resources for global impact.

Educate and raise a generation of Kingdom writers
who are called to spread the knowledge of God.

Support missionaries and missionary activities
around the world from a portion of sales.